Creating a Better World
First Edition

About This Book

This book is for those who want to create a better world for all people. If you want to do that, you're definitely in the right place. This book is based on the Day 1 Curriculum of the Hive Global Leaders Program.

An Experiment in Collaborative Creation

This book is being co-created and edited by the members of the Hive Community from twenty countries around the world in an experiment in collaborative creation. Anyone around the world can add comments directly to the digital version of the book at http://hive.org/course. These comments will be used to create the next edition. A new edition of this book will be published in print annually.

How Can I Join The Hive Community?

Hive is building a global community of people who are working to create a sustainable, abundant, and joyous world. We hold events that bring together leaders who want to create a better world. Learn more at www.hive.org.

Table of Contents

Part I: The Background

Part II: The Past

Part III: The Present

Part IV: The Future

Dedication

For the dreamers and all those working to create a sustainable, abundant, and joyous world. We believe in you.

Part I. The Background

Chapter 1: Empathy & Identity

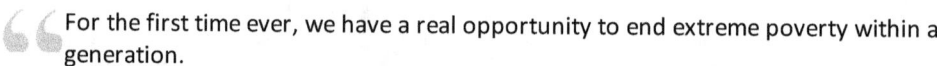 For the first time ever, we have a real opportunity to end extreme poverty within a generation.

- Jim Kim, President of the World Bank[31]

Empathy Circles

When a new baby is born, after about six months he is able to distinguish himself from others. If he pinches himself and it hurts, he stops doing it. His empathy circle has expanded to himself.

Soon thereafter, the infant develops a sense of family, the people around him taking care of him. His empathy circle has expanded again.

Around age 4, the young boy begins to go out into his community. Perhaps to pre-school or to day care. At this point, the boy begins to care for others in his community besides only his family. His empathy circle has grown once again.

Around age 5, the boy begins going to formal school and begins a lifelong process of seeing a connection with those he went to school with.

Perhaps around age 6, the boy may begin to learn about the country he lives in and any spiritual tradition his parents practice. His empathy circle grows again.

Most people today can empathize with members of their family, community, school, nation, and religious tradition.

The Usual Empathy Circles

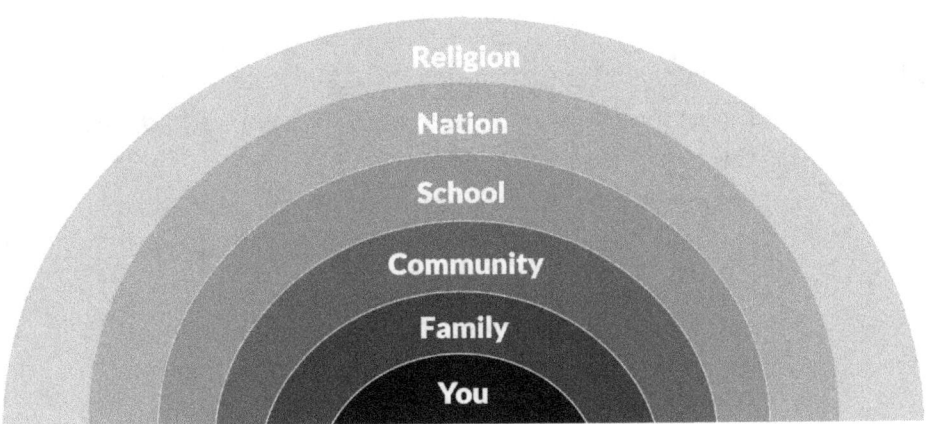

One key to our development, however, is to be able to move beyond the boundaries of national and religious affiliation so that our empathy can extend to reach all people, not just those who are closest to us.

Expanded Empathy Circles

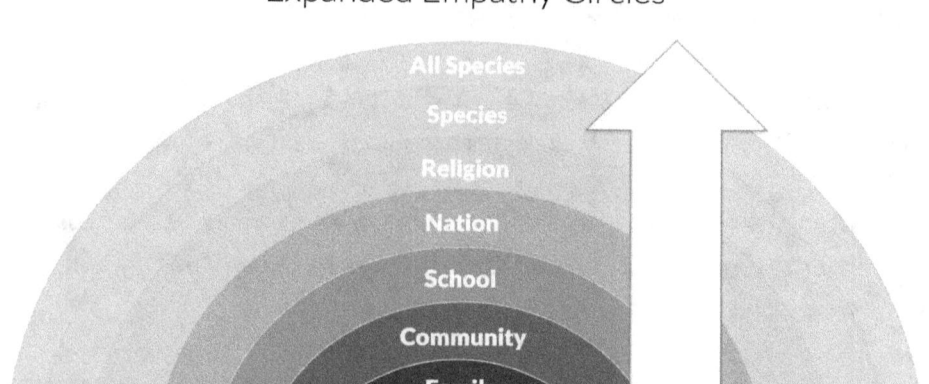

Why is this important? In the 20th century, humans lived in a disconnected world with two world wars and a very deadly battle between communism and capitalism.

We were separated from the rest of the world as there was no Wikipedia, Skype, WhatsApp, WeChat, Facebook, or Twitter. It was an "us vs. them" world in which politicians routinely painted the "other" as "lesser" for political or military gain.

George W. Bush's "Axis of Evil" speech during the 2002 State of the Union speech to build support for an upcoming war in Iraq in what was a classic example of using this us. vs. them mentality in rhetoric. When our political leaders activate our amygdala by claiming there is a threat, we are able to begin to dehumanize the threat, making it easier to justify killing the "other."

We saw that principle at work during World War II when Hitler referred to Jews as an inferior race. We saw that principle at work during the Rwandan genocide when Hutus referred to Tutsis as "inyenzi", a Kinyarwanda word meaning cockroaches.

Fortunately, today we are moving to a world that is connected like never before in which we see that the people living in Iraq, Iran, and North Korea (and all around the world) are often people just like you and us with the same hopes and dreams we all as human beings have.

As we will soon all be connected to a global communication tool, our hope is that we will be able to see that in fact we as humans are so similar and want the same thing--a happy life for ourselves and our families. We hope in this century, we can move beyond the anachronistic man-made false divisions of the 20th century and see that we really are all quite similar.

When political leaders controlled the information, they could misuse it to their benefit. Now, as we are coming close to ubiquitous global access to cloud-enabled smartphones with tools like Facebook, WeChat, Skype, and Twitter--we can begin to get information directly from each other rather than going through agencies and nation-states who may have distorted the information. This "seeing of each other" across cultures is key to the continuous expansion of empathy circles and a world based on peace rather than war.

We're mesmerized by the reality that for the first time in human history, our species is becoming connected. Not connected by radio like in the time of Wilson or connected by television like in the time of Truman, but no, connected together in a massively powerful, distributed, immediate, always on, peer-to-peer visual human network of trust and information. Transparency and openness leads to trust. This species-level change is what is leading to the opportunity now to catalyze a great turning in culture and bring the principles of compassion and respect for all people.

Challenge yourself. Are there any groups of people you don't like? Why? Where did that come from?

> A human being is a part of a whole, called by us the 'Universe,' a part limited in time and space. He experiences for himself, his thoughts and feelings, as something separated from the rest... Our task must be to free ourselves from this prison by widening our circles of compassion to embrace all living creatures and the whole of nature in its beauty. —*Albert Einstein*

Identity Labels

Growing up, you began to develop many identity labels. Perhaps you were a Jewish white man with one brother growing up in upstate New York as a Mets fan. Or maybe you were a Vietnamese Asian girl who eats vegan foods from Hat Yai and practices Buddhism. Let's look at how many identity labels are in just those two sentences.

1. Jewish
2. White
3. Boy
4. Brother
5. New Yorker
6. Mets Fan

1. Vietnamese
2. Asian
3. Female
4. Vegan
5. From Hat Yai
6. Buddhist

Everyone has identity labels about themselves. And that's okay. List out as many identity labels as you can for yourself in the box below.

Don't forget any identity labels for categories like nationality, gender, religion, sexual orientation, and any groups you're a part of. Go back and add more if you forgot any.

Now, how many did you come up with? Count them up.

Now, regardless of how many you came up with (most people can name at least 10), just know that within each identity label you have an affiliation with others like you.

The great opportunity, of course, is to be able to have empathy for all people, regardless of whether they are similar to you or not, and especially if they are different.

No matter what religion or spiritual tradition you look at, a key guideline is to be able to treat others well and care for others, especially those who may be the least well off or those who are very different than you.

Let's look at this concept in the various traditions:

Origin	Concept Name	Description
Judaism	*Tikkun Olam*	The concept of repairing the world
Sanskrit	*Ahimsa*	A philosophy of do no harm
Confucian	*Li*	A set of norms that teaches brotherliness and community
Islamic	*Ummah*	A perspective on a supranational community
Christian	*Golden Rule*	A practice of treating others as you want to be treated
South Africa	*Ubuntu*	A spirit of cooperation between people of all colors and creeds

In chapter two, we'll look at three principles of justice that can help us shape a better world.

Ch 2. The Three Principles

❝❝ For me, I am driven by two main philosophies: know more today about the world than I knew yesterday and lessen the suffering of others. You'd be surprised how far that gets you.

—Neil deGrasse Tyson

A Thought Exercise

Imagine yourself as a soul with five other souls around a campfire.

Let's do a famous thought exercise.

Imagine that you are a soul sitting around a campfire in a cave with five other souls. You haven't yet been born into your body. You don't know where you'll be born, what gender you'll be, what race you'll be, or what place in society your parents will have.

God tells you, "The six of you cannot be placed into your bodies until you agree on the basic principles for the world." God gives you one hour to discuss and agree to the principles of the world with the other souls before you must present them.

If you didn't know where you'll be born, your gender, your race, or how much money your parents will have, what basic principles for the world would you consider? Brainstorm some possibilities in the box below.

This thought exercise is based on the work of John Rawls (1921-2002), a 20th century philosopher who worked at Harvard. Rawls was focused on how to create a society that was just and fair.

In this thought exercise, the souls are in *The Original Position* (that is, before birth). The souls are behind what Rawls called a *Veil of Ignorance* as they do not yet know about the ethnicity, gender, or social status that they'll have after they are born.

In this original position, Rawls argues, the six souls are likely to agree on principles that were fair for all people.

In 1972, Rawls wrote in his book *Justice as Fairness*, "The most reasonable principles of justice are those everyone would accept and agree to from a fair position."

John Rawls believed that everyone is entitled to basic freedoms like freedom of speech, liberty, and the pursuit of happiness and that all citizens should have the same opportunity to hold office and influence elections.

The Three Principles

| 1 The Needs Principle | 2 The Rights Principle | 3 The Contribution Principle |

Here are three basic principles we came to when we put ourselves in the shoes of the six souls who didn't know their gender, skin color, socioeconomic status, or birthplace.

1. The Needs Principle
2. The Rights Principle
3. The Contribution Principle

Let's first look at each principle in order.

>   **The Needs Principle** - All people should have access to basic human needs like food, water, shelter, education, medicine, electricity, and the Internet.

As Rawls wrote, "**Each person has an equal claim to a fully adequate scheme of equal basic rights and liberties.**"

Today there are hundreds of millions of people in the world without access to these basic human needs. Let's look at this chart showing how many people still don't have access to these seven basic needs.

Basic human need	% Without	# Without	Source
1. Clean Water	10.6%	768M	UNICEF[1]
2. Sufficient Food	11.6%	842M	WFP[2]
3. Basic Shelter	13.9%	1000M	UNHCR[3]
4. Basic Literacy	12.8%	920M	UNESCO[4]
5. Basic Medicine	23.6%	1700M	WHO[5]
6. Electricity	18.1%	1300M	IEA[6]
7. The Internet	61.8%	4440M	World Bank[7]

Abraham Maslow arranged his *Hierarchy of Needs* in a pyramid with the most basic survival needs at the bottom and our higher needs for self-actualization and even self-transcendence at the top.

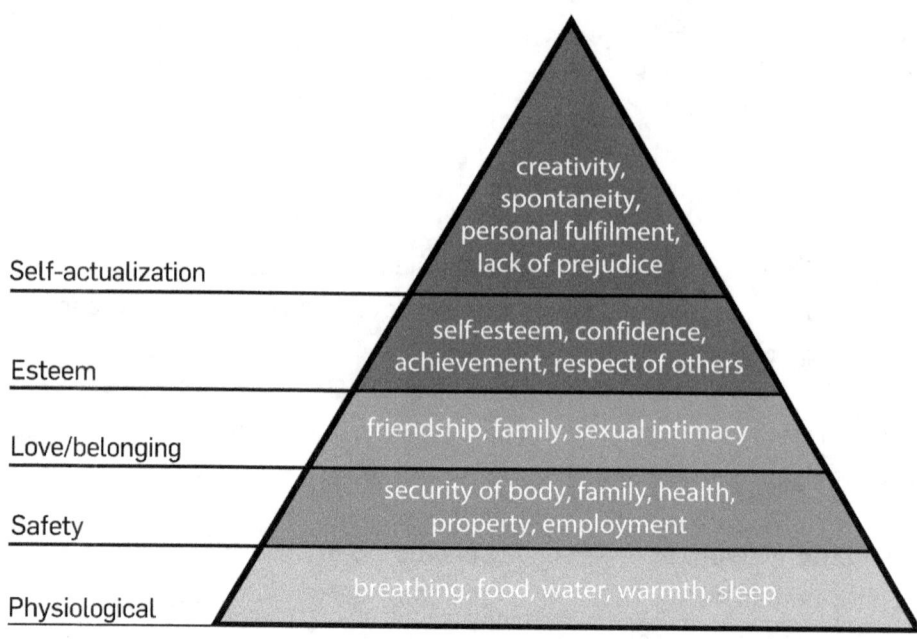

Turning the seven basic human needs above into a pyramid akin to Maslow's Hierarchy of Needs, it might look like the following image:

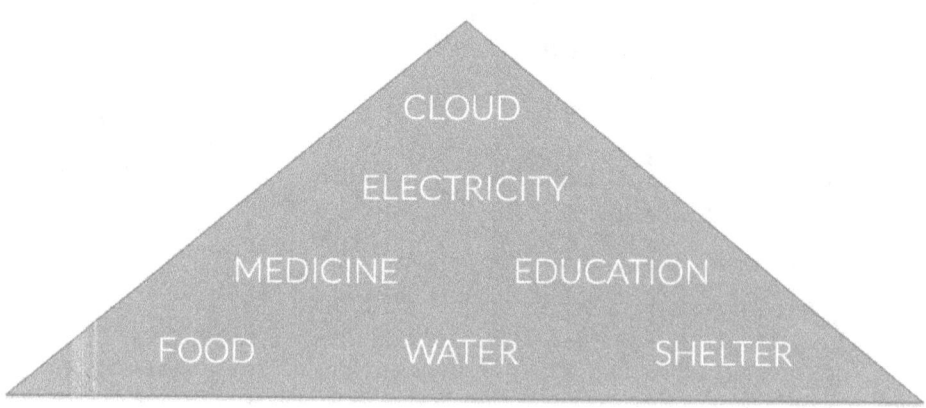

At the very bottom you have the most basic human needs, such as food, water, and shelter, and then a little higher up the pyramid we could add medicine and education, and at the top add electricity, and the Internet--allowing all of us to stay connected globally. In Maslow's time (1908-1970), the world wide web and mobile phones hadn't been invented, but these days both have become a key part to learning, global connection, and cultural understanding across borders.

Maslow's core insight was that these lower-level needs must be in place before a person's energy and attention is free to move up the pyramid and be able to create and innovate.

1. **Water** - Today, according to UNICEF, 780 million humans are without access to clean water. Most of us just turn on the tap and are not at all surprised when clean, drinkable water comes right out. In fact, we go to the bathroom in gallons of clean water every single day. Yet 10.6% of the world's population don't have access to clean water within 20 kilometers, sometimes even more.

2. **Food -** How many people don't have access to sufficient food to be able to power their bodies and provide the energy they need to live, to survive, to have a strong immune system? 842 million people, according to World Food Programme, more than twice the population of the United States.

3. **Shelter -** The third need is basic shelter. One billion people (that's 14% of the world's population) don't have access to sufficient shelter to shield themselves from the weather and to protect their families. There are about a billion people worldwide currently living in slums in urban areas that are densely populated and often don't have basic needs like sanitation, running water, and electricity.

4. **Education -** One of the factors that correlates with basic education is literacy. If you can't read or write, there are a lot of doors in this world that simply aren't open to you. There are still 920 million people globally, according to UNESCO, who do not have the ability to read or write (13% of the world).

5. **Medicine -** Next, let's take basic medicine. According to the World Health Organization, 1.7 billion human beings don't have access to lifesaving preventive measures and basic immunizations. We've made a lot of progress with reducing infant mortality, but if nearly one in four

humans don't have access to the most basic of medicines, we've still got a lot of work to do.

6. **Electricity** - Electricity was discovered in the 19th century. But more than a century later, we still have 1.3 billion people (18.5% of the world), according to the International Energy Agency, who do not have access to basic power. Imagine if you went home at night after school or work and as soon as the sun set, you couldn't read, you couldn't listen to music; you couldn't watch TV. That's the current case for 1.3 billion people. Imagine walking down your city street or neighborhood block in the middle of the night without street lights or going to turn on a light and realizing that in your city the electrical grid only works for 8 hours per day. This is the daily reality for hundreds of millions of people.

7. **Cloud Access -** Today there are about 2.8 billion people with access to the cloud. What that means is there are about 4.4 billion people (nearly 62% of humanity) who do not have access. Just think, for a moment, about what the Internet has already changed in your life—the access to opportunity, access to people, and access to information it has provided. So much happens when an individual who previously didn't have access to something as simple as Wikipedia suddenly gets online. When the innovative spirit within all of us suddenly gets connected to tens of thousands of years of human innovation, experience, and knowledge, magic can ensure. With this access, we can truly create anything we set our minds to. With the blueprints to build anything, do anything, and be anyone, so much rapid progress is possible. Fortunately, the marginal cost of providing additional Internet access is very low. We are excited by efforts like those by Internet.org, GoogleX, and the Facebook Connectivity Lab.

The Rights Principle

Next, let's look at the rights principle.

The Rights Principle - All people should have access to the same basic rights regardless of birthplace, gender, sexual orientation, or skin color.

There are still many examples of international and domestic laws that give people different rights based solely on birthplace, gender, sexual orientation, or skin color.

Here are a few examples where certain policies around the world don't match up with the rights principle that would call for all human beings to have the same human rights regardless of the latitude and longitudinal coordinates of birth (which is rather uncontrollable by a newborn baby).

- If you are born in England you have different abilities to travel to other countries than if you are born in Mali.

- If you are a woman living in Saudi Arabia you are not allowed to drive or work in jobs that interact with men.

- If you are gay and live in Uganda you can be killed for expressing your sexual orientation.

We believe these types of discrimination must stop and policies globally should be looked at through the lens of The Rights Principle. We believe that just because you are a woman or man or transgender individual, happen to be born in a certain place, happen to have a certain skin color, or happen to be straight or gay or bisexual that your basic rights as a human being should be the same.

The writers of the Declaration of Independence in 1776 wrote, "We hold these truths to be self-evident, that all men are created equal, that they are endowed by their Creator with certain unalienable Rights, that among these are Life, Liberty and the pursuit of Happiness."

Back in the late eighteenth century, when the framers wrote these words, they meant that only white male landowners were created equal. In one of the stranger anachronisms of the past, slaves in the United States were counted as only 3/5ths of a person after the Three-Fifths Compromise of 1787.

Over the past couple of centuries American citizens have wonderfully and continually expanded the definition of "all white men" to mean "all American people." Now it's time to expand what we mean by "all people are created equal" to actually mean every human being in the world.

In the 1950s and 60s, Martin Luther King Jr. shared his famous dream that his four children wouldn't be judged by the color of their skin but by the content of their character and that people of all colors could be treated equally. As much as we have progressed toward equality in the U.S. over the past sixty years, there's one part of King's dream that has not yet been realized: for all people globally to have equality of opportunity regardless of skin color, birthplace, gender, or sexual orientation. In 1967 before his death, King frequently wrote about his dream for true global equality of opportunity beyond the lens of just skin color.

Our dream of global equality of opportunity would mean a world in which everyone has at least their basic needs taken care of, so they can create, innovate, achieve, and contribute back to society. We think this is a world we can and should create in the decades ahead, and we think we'll have a safer and more secure world when everyone has access to basic human needs and rights.

The Contribution Principle

Finally, let's look at the contribution principle.

> *The Contribution Principle* - While we should all start off with equal opportunity, during life, those who contribute value to society should be rewarded.

It is important to ensure there was an incentive to contribute back to society beyond simply empathy and goodwill. All six souls should have equal basic rights and opportunities, but if one person chose to spend their lives contributing more to the benefit of society, then they should be rewarded as an incentive for the optimal outcomes for all.

When neurosurgeons, innovative entrepreneurial teams, and all those who work hard to hone their specialty and contribute their best gifts to humanity benefit, we all win. Incentives hugely matter to outcomes.

The Contribution Principle only works when all people have access to what they need at the bottom of the pyramid of needs to be able to be healthy and contribute. A system in which those who work hard and contribute value to humanity is good. A system in which many people don't have their basic needs sufficiently met to even be able to have a chance to contribute back to society isn't good. Thus the Contribution Principle only works hand in hand with the needs and rights principles.

Without the Needs Principle and Rights Principles in place first, you can have runaway inequality of income which has been shown to lead to less societal stability and less optimal outcomes for all--even for the wealthy. No matter the amount of money a wealthy person has, he or she is still at risk when so many in society remain without their basic needs met.

This risk comes from both localized crime as well as the spread of organizations like Al-Qaeda that often gain support by providing for the local needs of communities without their basic physiological and security needs met. Over the long run, a society in which we all have what we need to contribute back to society is a much better society for everybody.

Why do these principles matter? Well, many of you are going to be the future leaders of the world over the next forty years. The lenses through which you consider the global and national policies that may create the best outcomes are critically important.

So, as you influence global policy in the world in the decades ahead, consider how you can look through the lens of these three principles, *The Rights Principle*, *The Needs Principle*, and *The Contribution Principle.*

A Universal Declaration?

What if there were a simple document (like the Declaration of Independence) that established the rights of humans based on principles of fairness, which the United States and 48 other countries would adopt?

The reality is this document already exists and has been adopted by the USA and 48 other countries many years ago. It was created in 1948 by the United Nations. It's called the Universal Declaration of Human Rights. It was created in response to the horrors of World War II. Eleanor Roosevelt worked hard to make it happen.[8]

The Preamble begins with:

> "Whereas recognition of the inherent dignity and of the equal and inalienable rights of all members of the human family is the foundation of freedom, justice and peace in the world. Whereas disregard and contempt for human rights have resulted in barbarous acts which have outraged the conscience of mankind, and the advent of a world in which human beings shall enjoy freedom of speech and belief and freedom from fear and want has been proclaimed as the highest aspiration of the common people."

There are thirty articles in the Universal Declaration of Human Rights, beginning with "All human beings are born free and equal in dignity and rights. They are endowed with reason and conscience and should act towards one another in a spirit of brotherhood."

Take a look at the all thirty articles in the full Universal Declaration of Human Rights. It's a document that's rarely discussed in school, but it's one of the most important documents underlining the way the world can be in the future.

The Sustainable Development Goals

Back in the year 2000, 189 members of the United Nations committed to achieving the following eight Millennium Development Goals (MDGs) by the year 2015.

1. To eradicate extreme poverty and hunger
2. To achieve universal primary education

3. To promote gender equality and empowering women

4. To reduce child mortality rates

5. To improve maternal health

6. To combat HIV/AIDS, malaria, and other diseases

7. To ensure environmental sustainability

8. To develop a global partnership for development

The world has made substantial progress in all eight of these areas in the last 15 years.

In June 2012 in Rio De Janeiro, at the United Nations Conference on Sustainable Development, delegates agreed to create a set of global goals for 2015-2030, to be called the Sustainable Development Goals. The delegates created a document together called "The Future We Want" to lay the foundation for the new global goals.

Now, in 2014, the United Nations is convening a series of global conversations about the Sustainable Development Goals (SDGs), which will be put in place from 2015-2030. The UN is also conducting a global vote at MyWorld2015.org in which citizens from around the world can vote on their priorities for the next 15 years.

From the first 1.83 million votes on MyWorld2015, the top 6 global priorities were:

1. A good education
2. Better healthcare
3. An honest and responsive government
4. Better job opportunities
5. Affordable and nutritious food
6. Access to clean water and sanitation

It will be exciting to see what the Sustainable Development Goals will be for 2015-2030.

Over the next few decades, as Millennials come into the leadership positions across the world, we believe we actually will for the first time in human history create a world in which everyone has equal basic human rights, has access to basic needs like food, water, shelter, education, medicine, electricity, and the cloud, and has a sustainable planet to live on.

We believe every human being should have...

Access to

Food
Water
Shelter
Education
Medicine
Electricity
The Cloud

Equal status & rights

Under
Internationally
Accepted
And enforced law

An

&

Environmentally
Sustainable
World to
Live in

This is the way the world should be
and we can create this world in our lifetime

Recommended Chapter Resources:

Book: Justice as Fairness by John Rawls

Article: Stanford Encyclopedia of Philosophy: John Rawls

Video: Yale Course: The Rawlsian Social Contract

Video: On the Adoption of the Universal Declaration of Human Rights

UN Report: The Universal Declaration of Human Rights

UN Report: Realizing The Future We Want

Part II: The Past

Ch 3. The Story of Our Universe

"" The story really began 14 billion years ago with a tiny universe where everything was all in one place. Then the Big Bang—all the energy that has ever existed created in an instant. Gravity sculpted our universe. For billions of years stars and supernovas created all the elements we would eventually need. Then, an extreme Earth took shape and settled into just the right conditions to support life. As the planet evolved, life competed for energy and grew more and more complex.

—*The History of the World in Two Hours,* The History Channel

The Story of Our Universe

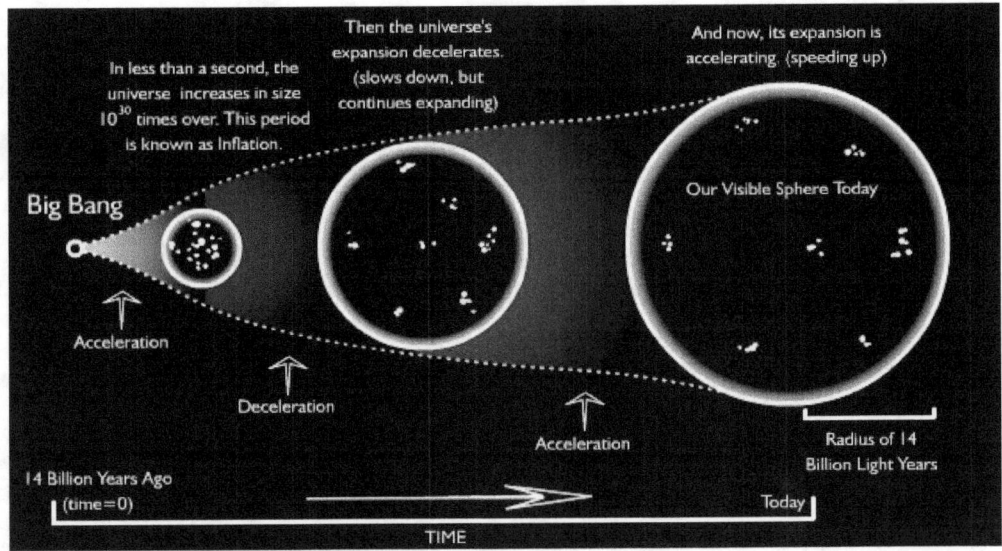

A description of the expanding universe, from the Lawrence Berkeley National Laboratory

We can only create wisely if we understand the context within which we are creating. So before we look further at how we can create a better world together in the decades ahead, let's take a few chapters to look at how the world we live in got here and the true temporality and delicacy of our spot on this planet. Feel free to skip ahead to chapter 6 if you're not a big history fan.

Just ponder for a moment the reality that human beings have been around 200,000 years, and yet the size of species has gone up 7x in just the last 200 years (0.1% of the time we've been around).

For the first time in human history, there is an unprecedented understanding of scientific knowledge, access to information, ability to communicate with one another, and awareness of the old and massive universe that we are a part of.

If we can become conscious of the fact that our place in space and time right now as human beings is extremely unique, much is possible in how we create the new guidelines of the world in the coming decades. We truly have the opportunity to remake the world into a sustainable, abundant, compassionate, joyous world in the decades ahead.

Let's jump into a review of Big History (history on a long time scale), looking first how our universe and planet got here and then looking at how we as human beings got here.

Scientists estimate how old our universe is by measuring its rate of expansion, called the Hubble Constant, and extrapolating backwards to the time when the universe would have had zero size. By this measure, it has taken the universe about 13.8 billion years to get to where we are today.

In 2009, the European Space Agency launched a probe into space called Planck which estimated the universe to be 13.798 billion years old.[9]

Soon after The Big Bang, the force of gravity began attracting matter together. Initial clouds of gas and dust formed causing pressure and heat to rise.

With extremely high temperatures in this early phase of our universe, hydrogen atoms fused into helium, which led to the formation of the first stars. These stars were massive spheres of plasma that converted hydrogen into helium.

To form planets, however, the universe needed a lot more elements than hydrogen and helium. The next elements to be created were lithium, carbon, oxygen, nitrogen, iron, and silicon. These elements came from star's continuous pressure and heat—enabling early solid planets to form.

The subsequent supernova explosions of stars at the end of their lives created additional elements like uranium, copper, zinc, and gold. The basic elements of the periodic table had formed, setting the stage for the formation of planets and our solar system.

4.6 billion years ago the star at the center of our solar system was born. Today, we call that star the Sun, originating from the Germanic mythological goddess Sunna.

The Story of Our Planet

The planet we live on, the third from the Sun, formed just over 4.5 billion years ago. Today we call this planet Earth, originating from the Germanic word "erde" meaning ground or soil.

The Earth began as a planet filled with molten lava mixed with various metals. The iron and nickel metals sank through the molten rock to the center of the still-forming Earth. This iron-nickel core of the planet created the Earth's magnetic field, protecting our planet from the sun's charged particles and setting up a key condition for life.

The early Earth had no moon. 4.5 billion years ago an object the size of Mars crashed into Earth at 25,000 miles per hour. The collision caused part of the planet to break off and form the moon. The collision that formed the moon tilted the planet, giving us seasons. The moon also slowed our rotation, increasing the number of hours in a day from six to twenty-four.

Imagine a world with six hour days and no seasons!

A Timeline of Earth

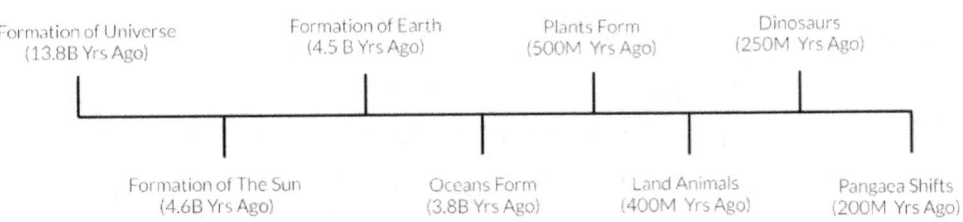

Formation of Universe (13.8B Yrs Ago) — Formation of Earth (4.5 B Yrs Ago) — Plants Form (500M Yrs Ago) — Dinosaurs (250M Yrs Ago)

Formation of The Sun (4.6B Yrs Ago) — Oceans Form (3.8B Yrs Ago) — Land Animals (400M Yrs Ago) — Pangaea Shifts (200M Yrs Ago)

Today, Earth rotates on its axis at about 1000 kph (a bit less if you're far from the equator) while revolving around the sun at 100,000 kph. We perceive we're standing still, but we're actually tiny human bodies attached by the force of gravity to a planet that is moving in space at 29 kilometers (16 miles) per second. You are hundreds of kilometers away in space from the spot you were in when you began reading this sentence! We don't feel the motion of course because it is constant and only acceleration and deceleration is felt, not constant motion.

3.8 billion years ago, the oceans had just formed and the planet had cooled. Hydrogen, oxygen, carbon, and nitrogen combined to form the key substances for life. The first life forms soon emerged in our oceans in the form of single-celled bacteria or prokaryotes. These prokaryotes figured out how to consume the sun's energy to live and emitted oxygen as their waste product.

As oxygen permeated our atmosphere, some bacterial life forms learned to live on oxygen—which was more efficient for obtaining energy than direct photosynthesis—enabling the evolution of more complex life forms. 500 million years ago, oxygen levels became high enough for more complex vertebrate animals like fish to evolve during the period known as the Cambrian explosion.

With oxygen, came an ozone layer, protecting the planet from radiation. Around 400 million years ago, animals began living on land—first amphibians, then reptiles with water-filled eggs, and then mammals.

The continents were connected together in one land mass called Pangea. They began shifting apart about 200 million years ago, forming the Americas, Eurasia, Africa, and Oceania and separating into two major landmasses—only briefly connected by the Bering Strait during the ice ages.

During this time, dinosaurs became the most advanced species on the planet for 160 million years. They reigned supreme until a six-mile-wide asteroid hit the planet 66 million years ago, leaving behind the Chicxulub Crater near the Yucatan Peninsula in the Gulf of Mexico.

This massive asteroid created a dust cloud which blocked out the sun, reduced temperatures, prevented many plants from completing photosynthesis, and led to the extinction of land-based dinosaurs, allowing for the evolution of more complex primates and later on, humans.

That brings us to our next chapter, about the story of humanity and how we ended up here on this planet.

Chapter 4: The Story of Our Species

66 A human being is a part of the whole, called by us "Universe", a part limited in time and space. He experiences himself, his thoughts and feelings as something separated from the rest — a kind of optical delusion of his consciousness. The striving to free oneself from this delusion is the one issue of true religion. Not to nourish the delusion but to try to overcome it is the way to reach the attainable measure of peace of mind.

- Albert Einstein, February 12, 1950[10]

The Story of Humanity

It's important to understand how we ended up on this wonderful planet and how our civilization has gotten to this rather unique and rapidly changing point in history.

Before we look at how we can memetically evolve culture and create a stronger human tribe together in the decades ahead, let's look at how we've ended up here, on this fast moving pale blue dot.

It's fascinating to realize our lives (everything we have ever known) have been less than 0.01% of human history and that human beings as a species have only been around for 0.004% of the Earth's history.

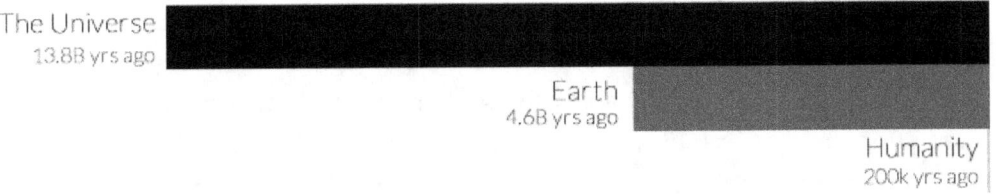

We truly are a blip in the history of this pale blue dot in the Milky Way. Looking at a different time scale, if the Earth had been around for 1000 years, humans would have only been around for just the last 14 days.

In this chapter, we take a rapid look into how the basis of today's advanced civilization has formed. This chapter is meant to be a quick overview of our background designed to prepare us for looking at how we can together create a better world in the future. We jump quickly here through million of years.

Let's begin.

We are sentient creatures with many millions of years of evolution guiding our physiology and brains. Our early ancestors, primates, first came onto the scene around 85 million years ago. Initially, these small primates were not much of a match for the fiercer dinosaurs.

However, after the six-mile wide asteroid hit the Earth 66 million years ago, these fierce reptiles were wiped out, setting the stage for the rapid evolution of other mammals and primates and laying the groundwork for humanity.

It is a turn of chance that such a catastrophe enabled for us to develop. Who knows what sentient life will be on this planet 50 million years from now after the next major exogenous event impacts our world. Thus, Elon Musk's vision to spread humanity to planets outside of Earth and provide an insurance plan for our species is of great importance.

By seven million years ago, primates who could walk upright began walking about the grasslands of Eastern Africa. Imagine the grasslands of Ethiopia with upright walking primates struggling to survive the many threats of the open Savannahs.

Walking upright created a natural advantage for these new primates and hands were freed up for new tasks. It was here that our primitive amygdala formed, creating the rapid decision making ability to choose between "fight" or "flight."

Around five million years ago, the Hominini tribe of bipedal human-like ancestors diverged from the Panini tribe of chimpanzees. Three million years later, our *homo habilis* (able man) ancestors came onto the scene. The Homo habilis had a cranial capacity just less than half of the size of modern humans and began using tools like stone flakes for eating.

A Timeline of Humanity

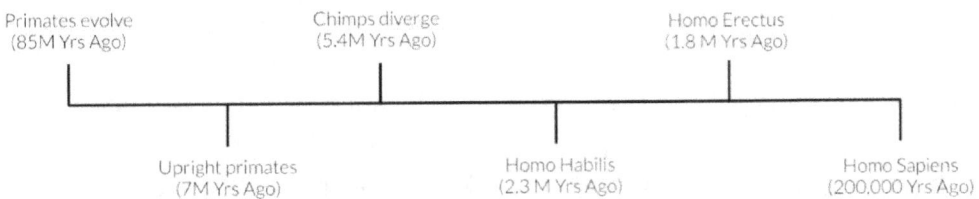

Primates evolve
(85M Yrs Ago)

Chimps diverge
(5.4M Yrs Ago)

Homo Erectus
(1.8 M Yrs Ago)

Upright primates
(7M Yrs Ago)

Homo Habilis
(2.3 M Yrs Ago)

Homo Sapiens
(200,000 Yrs Ago)

Following the homo habilis was the *homo erectus* (upright man), a species with fossils dating back 1.8 million years. The homo erectus evolved larger brains and were the first to use fire around 400,000 years ago in the early Stone Age.

With fire we were able to use it to cook, break down food, and consume more calories than before. Modern *homo sapiens* (wise man) finally arrived 200,000 years ago in the Middle Paleolithic Age. In homo sapiens, the larynx and hyoid bone descended, making speech possible, leading to the rapid evolution of sharing and learning that has led us to the rapidly advancing species we are today.

The First Cities

Eridu was formed by the Sumerians in 5400 BCE near the banks of The Euphrates in Mesopotamia. Depicted here by artist Balage Balogh.

One can not overemphasize how important agriculture was in the development of humanity. Around 10,000 BCE, the first farming of plants occurred. Instead of having to continually move around as nomadic tribes, seeking new places to hunt and to gather, we could live for a long time in one place, allowing us to form larger stationary communities and cities, which set the stage for the development and spread of human knowledge.

Farming changed everything for humans, enabling the formation of stable rather than migratory populations and laying the foundation for human populations grow. Dependable food supplies allowed people to build permanent houses and settle in one area. As methods of agriculture improved and more people chose to stay stationary on the land, the first towns and cities were formed, followed by the development of the first laws, monetary instruments, and markets.

Arguably the world's first city, Eridu, was formed on the banks of the Euphrates River around 5400 BCE. By 3,000 BCE, settlements and cities had formed all over Sumeria near modern day Iraq. By that time, the city of Uruk along the banks of the Euphrates River was home to 50,000 people in an amount of space that would have previously supported just one hunter-gatherer. Humans had become much more efficient at generating the food and energy necessary to support their community.[11]

The Middle East's fertile crescent between the Tigris and the Euphrates had just the right mix of plants and animals to sustain the first foundations of civilization. As more people moved into these stable communities, one of the most important advances took place. The beginning of specialization. With specialization of human labor, instead of each tribe hunting and gathering their food, different individuals within each tribe would become experts at certain tasks, such as farming, hunting, gathering, fishing, cooking, tool-making, shelter-building, or clothes-making.

As some individuals in a community focused on one activity, they got much better at it, speeding up the pace of innovation. As different people got better at different tasks through specialization, they were then able to exchange with one another for the various goods and services needed, increasing the benefits for all. This led to rapid advancement in many fields as experts developed and then shared their learnings across tribes.

5,000 years ago, human civilizations began to spring up near other rivers like the Nile, the Indus, and the Yellow and Yangtze. In these first cities, writing was developed to keep track of crops. In this period, the first armies developed and the first city governments were formed. Agricultural settlements had put humanity on a rapidly developing path toward intellectual and scientific advancement.

As settlements increased in size, new social institutions such as religious centers, courts, and marketplaces developed. The advent of towns produced further specialization, creating jobs in tool-making, pottery, carpentry, wool-making, and masonry, among others. The specialist created items faster and of a better quality than each family making its own, increasing standards of living.

This specialization set the stages for the creation of money and the invention of markets and trade--the initial force that brought the various cultures together across great distances.

Expanding Nodes of Human Connection

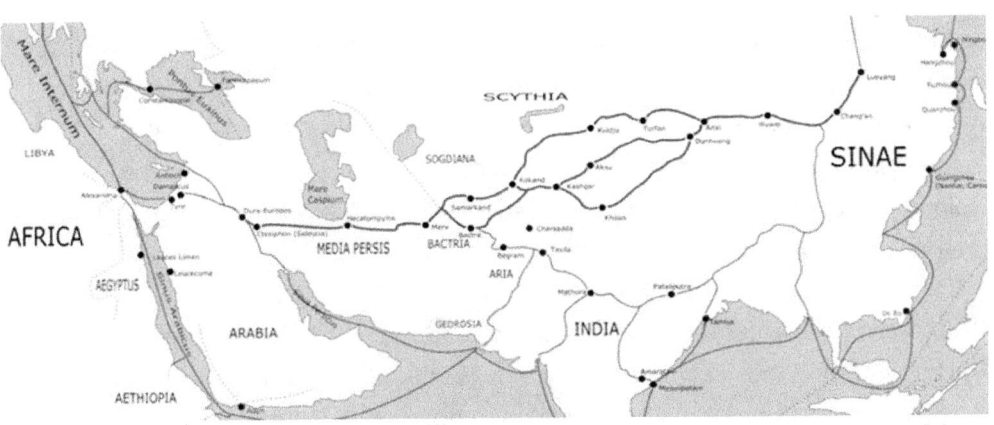

Early trade routes along the Silk Road around 100 CE

One of the earliest known instances of humans trading comes from New Guinea around 17,000 BCE, where locals exchanged goods for obsidian, a black volcanic glass used to make hunting arrowheads.[12]

Early trade consisted of barter of one good for another. There was a big problem with bartering however. In order for a trade to take place, both parties had to want what the other party had. This *coincidence of wants* often did not happen.

Thus, the demands of trade gave rise to money, which could be used to enable exchange even if both parties didn't have exactly what the other was after. Silver rings or bars are thought to have been used as money in Ancient Iraq before 2000 B.C. Early forms of money called *specie* would be often be commodities like seashells, tobacco leaves, large round rocks, or beads.[13]

While credit and paper money did not yet exist, the invention of money over four thousand years ago was of crucial importance to the world we live in today. The use of money, a medium to store value and enable exchange, has greatly enhanced our world, our lives, our potential, and our future.

As new cities developed and trade routes sprang up ships were built to carry trade over the seas. Networks and hubs soon formed along waterways and more complex structures emerged. Great Pyramids were built in Cairo. Temples were built in Sumeria.

Around 2000 BCE, the process of separating iron from iron ore was discovered, leading to advances in warfare as bronze weapons were replaced with the stronger iron. Around 600 BCE, human warriors with iron weaponry on horseback led to the creation of the first empires, broad lands conquered violently by the armies of people like Genghis Khan, Alexander the Great, Attila the Hun, and Ashoka the Great.

One can wonder whether these empires would have been less prone to warfare had they been able to communicate with other human beings via telephones and the internet and developed bonds of trust and greater compassion for each other and seen how their peoples could have actually worked together for both sides to benefit.

As trade routes and empires expanded, salt from Africa reached Rome, rice traveled from China across Asia, and the secrets of making paper were transferred from China to Europe. Arab traders brought coffee, lemons, and oranges into Europe for the first time.

Around 800, gunpowder was discovered in China when carbon and sulphur were combined with potassium nitrate. Around the year 1200, an Italian trader named Leonardo Fibonacci brought the standard system of numbers that we still use today from Arabia to Europe.

Long-distance trade was expanding and new worlds of foreign spices, oriental treasures, and luxurious silks were discovered. After weathering a Black Death in the 14th century, Europe emerged by expanding trade to new levels and building the foundation for the start of the competitive market economy we know today.

The Aztecs, Mayans, and Incan empires formed in the Americas separated from the rest of the world since the Bering Strait land bridge had submerged around 8000 BCE.

The sea voyages of Leif Erikson and Christopher Columbus connected Europe and the Americas, bringing guns, horses, and diseases. With the importance of Atlantic trade, power shifted toward the West in the coming centuries as Europeans colonized and laid the foundations for a globalized world. The reconnection of the hemispheres marked a key point for our species.

The Creation of Vibrant Markets

An 1877 painting by Gustav Bauernfeind of the early markets in Jaffa

With a population spurt starting in the 15th century, cities, markets, and the volume of trade grew. Banking, initially started by Ancient Mesopotamians, grew to new heights and complexities; the guild system expanded; and the idea that a business was an impersonal entity, with a separate identity from its owner, started to spread.[14]

Silver imports from the new world drove expanded trade and bookkeepers created standardized principles for keeping track of a firm's accounts based on Luca Pacioli's accounting advances. Early entrepreneurs, called merchants and explorers, began to raise capital, take risks, and stimulate economic growth. Capitalism had begun.

Early on in the history of markets, the idea of monetary gain was shunned and shamed by many. The practice of usury, charging interest on loans, was banned by the Church. Jobs were usually assigned by tradition and caste.

Innovation was often stifled and efficiency was forcefully put down, sometimes punishable by death. In sixteenth-century England, when mass production in the weaving industry first came about, the guildsmen protested. An efficient workshop containing two hundred looms and butchers and bakers for the workers was outlawed by the King under the pretense that such efficiency reduced the number of available jobs.

As an example of the madness, makers of innovative shirt buttons in France in the late 1600s were fined and searched and the importation of printed calico textiles cost the lives of 16,000 people.[15]

> The pre-capitalist era saw the birth of the printing press, the paper mill, the windmill, the mechanical clock, the map, and a host of other inventions. The idea of invention itself took hold; experimentation and innovation were looked upon for the first time with a friendly eye.
>
> - Ronald Heilbroner, *The Worldly Philosophers*

As we entered the Enlightenment in the 17th and 18th century and focused on rationality, science, and reason, the world began to see that innovation was generally a good thing, making lives better, reducing poverty around the world, making food available to all, and that efficiency was a path toward a higher standard of a living.

A Timeline of Pre-Industrial Human Innovation

Fire (400,000 BCE) - The controlled use of fire was an invention in the early Stone Age, with some of the earliest evidence dating back to hundreds of thousands of years ago. It's not exactly certain when fire was first being used by humans, but most research puts it somewhere between 200,000 and 600,000 years ago. Fire allowed humans to cook their meat, enabling the development of higher calorie diets and the expansion of brain size.

Language (100,000 BCE) - True semantic, phonetic language was first being used around 100,000 BCE, making it a lot easier to pass on how-to knowledge from generation to generation and speeding the spread of innovation.

Farming (15,000 BCE) - The first animal domestication began taking place around 15,000 BCE, and around 10,000 BCE, the first domestication of plants.

Food Preservation (12,000 BCE) - Food preservation began around 12,000 BCE as civilizations in the Middle East extended the life of their foods through drying them in the sun. With the ability keep food edible beyond the time that it would naturally go bad, and store it for the future, time and energy were made available to work on other things besides simply farming, hunting, and gathering, enabling a great advance in our ability to specialize and trade. With greater specialization and trade came a substantial increase in the variety of tools and goods available.

Bronze (4000 BCE) - The science of metallurgy began around 4400 BCE when human civilizations began to use copper and silver, and soon thereafter we figured out how to merge copper and tin to form bronze.

The Ship (4000 BCE) - The ancient Egyptians were making wooden sailboats around 4000 BCE and around 1200 BCE the Phoenicians and the Greeks began to make even bigger sailing ships. The advent of the ship was a huge step forward for humanity because it was one of the first forms of transport that enabled commerce to begin happening between different parts of the world.

The Wheel (3400 BCE) - The next significant step in the history of innovation came with the creation of the wheel, sometime between 3300 and 3500 BCE. Scientists know this due to the discovery in southern Poland of a depiction of a wheeled vehicle on a clay pot.

Money (3000 BCE) - The next critically important innovation that contributed to the development of a strong human civilization was money. Around 3000 BCE, the Sumerians were one of the first societies (if not *the* first) to begin using money to help the ease of commerce and exchanging of goods, replacing the barter system.

Iron (3000 BCE) - Around 3000 BCE we found an even stronger substance called iron, which gave rise to a new age of human history.

Written Language (2900 BCE) - Although language had been around for tens of thousands of years, the invention of written language was extremely important because it made written records and numerical calculations possible. The first recorded written language was Sumerian cuneiform, which started around 2900 BCE.

Steel (2000 BCE) - Steel is an alloy between iron and carbon, and one of the strongest substances we know. The earliest known steel was excavated in Western Asia and dated to be about 4,000 years old. The Spartans used steel extensively around 650 BCE, as did the Chinese from 400 BCE, and the Romans.

The Legal System (1780 BCE) - In 1780 BCE, Hammurabi, the sixth king of Babylon, was one of the first to write down a formalized code of laws. He created a structure that enabled his people to understand what the societal norms were. Other examples include the Egyptian Book of the Dead, the Ten Commandments, the Twelve Tables of Rome, and the Book of Leviticus—early legal systems that enabled society to tackle dispute resolution at a lower cost and create an understanding of what the norms are. These systems helped create amazing advancement in our ability to conduct commerce in a frictionless environment.

The Alphabet (1050 BCE) - The first "true alphabet" (containing vowels as well as consonants) was created by the Phoenicians around 1050 BCE. Many modern alphabets evolved from the Phoenician alphabet.

Water Power (200 BCE) - The next great innovation, around 200 BCE, was water power—first used in the Fertile Crescent area in the Middle East. This breakthrough enabled enormous transformations in our ability as a species to harness power, and water power continued to be used into the nineteenth century, when water-powered mills were still common in England and New England, and is still used to this day for hydroelectric power.

Paper (105) - Moving into the common era calendar, we saw the creation of paper, which was first used by the Chinese in around the year 105. Around the sixteenth century, wood pulp paper became more widely used, replacing rag paper. With wood paper, knowledge could spread much more easily.

Movable Type (1040) - Advancing about 900 years, we had the creation of movable type. While many people think that movable type began in 1436 with Gutenberg's printing press, it actually goes back to imperial China in year 1040. Later, when Gutenberg invented his press, he was able to use special inks and tin, lead, and antimony to mass-produce books and get content to the educated folks of Europe in the fifteenth century.

The Microscope (1592) - The microscope was an extremely important invention that has led to the more recent breakthroughs in the understanding of nanotechnology and the understanding of atomic structure. Back in 1592, Dutch spectacle makers Zacharias and Hans, a father and son team, discovered that nearby objects appeared greatly enlarged when looking through a specially shaped lens, creating the first known microscope.

Electricity (1600) - Going forward to 1600, English scientist William Gilbert coined the term electricity, which originated from the Greek word for amber. Later, in 1752, Ben Franklin showed that lightning and the spark from amber were one and the same substance: electricity.

The Telescope (1608) - In 1608, Hans Lippershey created a convex lens and concave eyepiece that enabled the creation of the telescope. The next year, Galileo Galilei built on these early designs to create a much more powerful telescope that enabled us to truly see the heavens and understand our place in the universe.

Ch 5. The Accelerating Industrial Age

" " Just when it seemed we had reached our human limits we found the energy and technology to carry us into the future. On Earth, the seeds of the past have bloomed into a present filled with energy creativity. The stories of billions of lives have played out against a backdrop of a universe almost too vast to comprehend. In everything that we do, in all that we are, we remain living monuments to the past, as we continue to make history every day.

—*The History of the World in Two Hours*, The History Channel

The Industrial Revolution

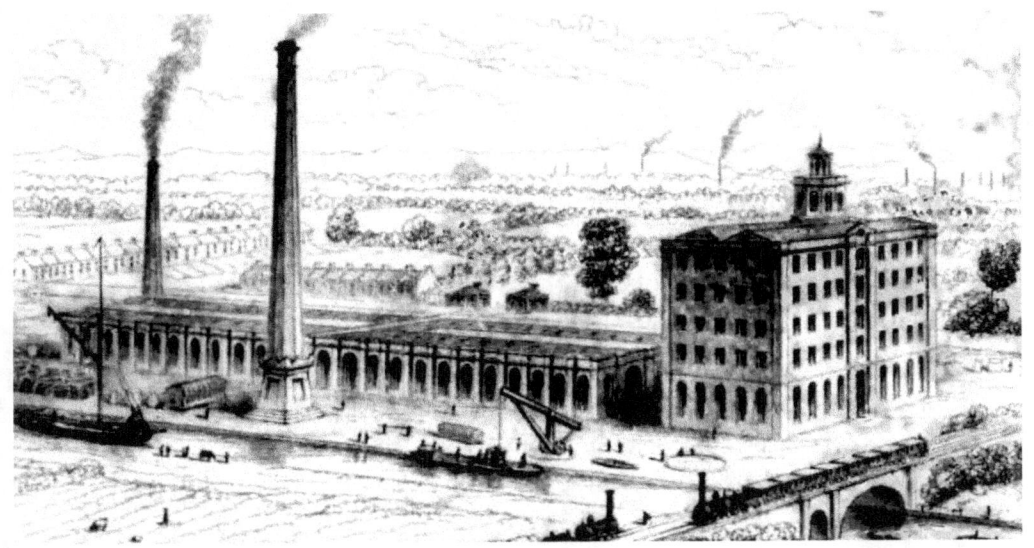

The Bridgewater Foundry in 1839 near Liverpool, England, one of the earliest factories to use an assembly line system

Now we're moving into looking at how the global system that we know of today has developed over the last couple centuries. While many believe that what we have today is the way it's always been, the current structure of the capitalist industrial complex has developed only in the last 0.1% of human history.

In the next 50 years we have the ability to shift this industrial model to one of sustainable production in which all people can have what they need to contribute back to society. We have the opportunity to reimagine capitalism and the incentive structures that drive behavior within it.

Looking backwards at recent history, the story of the last 200 years is one of machines, markets, and the rapid expansion of human population from 1 billion to over 7 billion.

The Industrial Age arguably began in 1712 with the invention of Thomas Newcomen's steam engine in Devon, Britain. But it wasn't until James Watt's steam engine in 1763 that things really got moving, enabling work to be done through the movement of pistons rather than the movement of muscle.

New schools of thought sprung up in the 18th century that promoted commerce as the source of wealth, rather than the older misguided mercantilist notion of the hoarding of gold being the path to national wealth.

Adam Smith was one of the first to capture and explain the dynamic essence of the marketplace in his 1776 work *An Inquiry into the Nature and Causes of the Wealth of Nations*. Smith explained that self-interest acts as a guiding force toward the work society desires.

> It is not from the benevolence of the butcher, the brewer, or the baker that we expect our dinner, but from their regard to their self-interest.
>
> —*Adam Smith, The Wealth of Nations*

By the time of Adam Smith's death in 1790, the nascent Industrial Revolution had already reared its head. The effects of the Renaissance, the humanist movement, and the Enlightenment's focus on science and empiricism would translate into the launch of a movement that would impact the world as none before it had.

A new agricultural revolution worked hand in hand with the Industrial Revolution to surprise the Malthusian fans. New crops like corn and potatoes came from the Americas into Europe. New technologies like the seed drill and new methods like better fertilization enabled greatly expanded outputs.

More agricultural output meant that more food was able to feed urban industrial laborers. And the railroad enabled agricultural outputs to be transported across countries quickly and easily. The invention of the internal combustion engine around 1860 combined with the discovery of petroleum in 1859 enabled new equipment like combines and tractors that increased yields further.

Timeline of The 19th Century

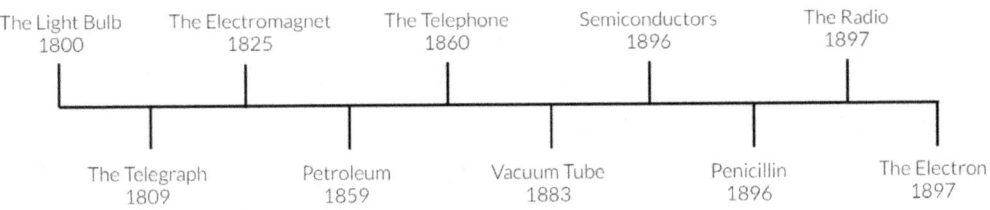

| The Light Bulb | The Electromagnet | The Telephone | Semiconductors | The Radio |
| 1800 | 1825 | 1860 | 1896 | 1897 |

| The Telegraph | Petroleum | Vacuum Tube | Penicillin | The Electron |
| 1809 | 1859 | 1883 | 1896 | 1897 |

It was this Industrial Revolution—often dirty, hierarchical, and cruel—that prompted Marx's thoughts of communism and created robber barons and industrial titans. It was this same revolution, however, that led to the development of the innovations, technology, and standards of living we have today.

From the Industrial Revolution, the concept of mass production and economies of scale came about. Bigness, trusts, and vertical integration became the key to riches at that time. It was Andrew Carnegie and J. P. Morgan in steel, John D. Rockefeller and Frank Kenan in oil, and Henry Ford in automobiles. While some of these titans had questionable ethics, no one can deny that they were innovators. They forged alliances, developed new ways of doing business, and created efficiency across industries.

It was the combination of energy and engine that freed man from the constraints of muscle power, making the Atlantic world the greatest military power and laying the foundations for the locomotive, the internal combustion engine, the automobile, and the discovery of oil. The telegraph and telephone connected humanity around the world. With electricity, we lit up the night.

A Timeline of Industrial Age Innovation

The Engine (1712) - The steam engine was first invented by Thomas Newcomen in 1712 building on the ideas on Denis Papin and Thomas Savery.

Steam power was tremendously important to the development of seafaring navigation and to powering the machinery that drove the industrial revolution. The internal combustion engine followed, first made commercially successful by Etienne Lenoir in 1858.

The Light Bulb (1800) - In 1800, Humphry Davy, an English scientist, created the first light bulb. It was improved in 1879 by Thomas Edison, who discovered that a certain type of carbon filament, when placed in bulb without oxygen, could glow for 40 hours. Later on, Edison would create a bulb that could last for over 1,500 hours—a tremendous advancement in our ability as a society to be able to do things even after the sun has set.

The Telegraph (1809) - In 1809, the first crude telegraph was invented in Bavaria by Samuel Soemmering, and in 1828 the first telegraph in the United States was invented by Harrison Dyer. It was, of course, Samuel Morse, creator of the Morse code, who invented the telegraph communication system that ended up succeeding commercially.

The Electromagnet (1825) - In 1825, the electric magnet was discovered by British inventor William Sturgeon. His first magnet was an iron horseshoe wrapped with copper wire. When he passed an electric current through the wire, the 7 oz. horseshoe became a magnet and could lift nine pounds. Electromagnets went on to be used in motors, generators, loudspeakers, hard drives, MRI machines, and particle accelerators.

Petroleum (1859) - In 1859, petroleum was discovered. The first natural gas well was created in Ohio and the first oil well was created and the first oil refined in Pennsylvania. Petroleum was one of the most efficient substances in terms of the amount of energy that could be expended per ounce of liquid when burned. The discovery of petroleum, of course, led to the gas-powered car half a century later as well as a substantial increase of carbon dioxide in the atmosphere.

The Telephone (1860) - In 1860, the telephone was invented by Johann Philipp Reis. He was the first to produce a functioning electromagnetic device that could transmit understandable sounds. Sixteen years later, Alexander Graham Bell received the first patent for telephones and invented the first commercially successful telephone.

The Vacuum Tube (1883) - In 1883, Thomas Edison discovered that an electrical current doesn't need a wire through which to move—it could actually travel through gas or a vacuum. In 1893, ten years later, Lee De Forest invented the Audion, which could control the flow of and amplify the current—an innovation that became critically important to telecommunication later on in the twentieth century.

Semiconductors (1896) - In 1896, the first semiconductors were discovered. A semiconductor is simply material that has electrical conductivity due to flowing electrons. Jagadish Chandra Bose, the founder of the Bose Corporation, was the first to apply semiconductors for commercial purposes around 1896. Today, silicon serves as the main component for most commercially produced semiconductors, the reason that the area between San Francisco and San Jose became known as Silicon Valley.

Penicillin (1896) - In 1896, the French medical student Ernest Duchesne originally discovered the antibiotic properties of Penicillium, however his research went mostly unnoticed. It took until 1928 for Scottish biologist Alexander Fleming to re-discovered penicillin. Penicillin enabled doctors to fight bacterial infections, save lives, and cure syphilis, gangrene and tuberculosis.

The Radio (1897) - The next great invention was the radio. In 1897, Nikola Tesla applied for and received the first radio system patent after demonstrating it the year before at the World's Fair. Radio took advantage of the amazing invisible parts of the electromagnetic spectrum to transmit information through waves. Today, we take it for granted that signals can travel invisibly through the air, but 130 years ago it was quite radical to demonstrate that there were things that we could not see that were still real. In fact, the visible part is only a very small fraction of the full electromagnetic spectrum.

The Electron (1897) - That same year, 1897, J. Thomson discovered the electron. An electron is a negatively charged subatomic particle and it's the primary carrier of electricity, which of course has revolutionized the world in the last 115 years.

Quantum Physics (1900) - The history of quantum physics is quite fascinating. It began with a number of discoveries going back all the way to 1838 with Michael Faraday's discovery of cathode ray tube, and included 1887's discovery by Heinrich Hertz of the photoelectric effect. But the real beginning of quantum physics was arguably in 1900 with Max Planck's quantum hypothesis: that any energy-radiating atomic system can be divided into individual energy elements. Using that research in 1905, Albert Einstein theorized and later proved that light is made up of individual quantum particles which were later termed photons by Gilbert Lewis.

The Airplane (1903) - We saw the invention of the airplane by the Wright brothers, Orville and Wilbur, on the North Carolina coast with the first successful flight of a manned machine occurring on December 17, 1903.

Television (1926) - The creation of television happened in 1926, but there were many inventions that led up to it, including the discovery of the photoconductivity of selenium in 1873 by Willoughby Smith and the 1884 invention of the scanning disk by Paul Nipkow. It was John Logie Baird who created the first televised moving images in 1926. Ten years later, the British Broadcasting Corporation (BBC) broadcast the first public television show.

The Transistor (1947) – 1947 saw the creation of the transistor. A transistor is a device that's used to amplify and switch electronic signals. It's extremely important in the ability to exchange information over a distance. Once we could amplify electronic signals we could have global telecommunications. In 1906, Lee De Forest had developed the triode in a vacuum tube that could amplify signals, which had helped overseas telephone calls be made for the first time, but it was in 1947 at AT&T that Bill Shankly and his team created the first semiconductor transistor. Of course, it was Bill Shankly who later founded Shankly Semiconductor, out of which Fairchild Semiconductor and later Intel were born.

Ch. 6 A Turbulent 20th Century

> If we take the view that Germany must be kept impoverished, and its children starved and crippled, vengeance I dare predict will not limp. Nothing can delay that final war that will destroy the civilization and progress of our generation.
>
> > - John Maynard Keynes, *The Economic Consequences of the Peace (1919)*

Three Terrible Wars

The New York City Skyline in 1932

In the 20th century, we used the new tools of the Industrial Age to create major scientific advances. The century was filled with technological innovation as well as an ideological struggle between centrally planned economies based on state control and distributed planning economies based on the competitive market economy.

The century was marked by three major wars--World War I, World War II, and the Cold War (which wasn't 'cold' at all).

From two atomic bombs dropped on Japan to Mao's Great Leap Forward to the Khmer Rouge in Cambodia to the Rwandan Genocide it was a turbulent century that brought approximately 200 million deaths from war.

The first World War began in 1914 when Archduke Franz Ferdinand was shot by Serbian nationalist Gavrilo Princip in Sarajevo. Should you ever have any doubt that the world of today is substantially more peaceful and interconnected than the world of 1914, read the July Ultimatum between the Austro-Hungarian Empire and Serbia. It was a world of miscommunication and mistrust in which national and religious identity often trumped human identity and the broader empathy circles and better communication tools we have today.

World War I ended with the Treaty of Versailles in Paris 1919. With the treaty, the Allied Forces compelled Germany to pay reparations roughly equivalent to $440 billion (in today's dollars), strongly against the wishes of British economist John Maynard Keynes, who saw the payments as excessive and counterproductive to continued peace.

In 1922, the Soviet Union was formed following the Bolshevik Revolution and a Russian Civil War. The Lenin-led USSR, influenced by the ideas of German philosopher Karl Marx, implemented a centrally planned economic model in which prices, outputs, and professions were determined by the government instead the market.

Against the background of this new Soviet economic model, in the U.S. the Dow Jones Industrial Average dropped 89% between 1929 and 1932 from a high of 380.3 in 1929 to a low of 42.8. U.S. GDP dropped from $103.6 billion in 1929 to $56.4 billion in 1932.[16] Unemployment in the U.S. rose from 4% in 1928 to 24% in 1933.

Keynes' laid out the recovery plan for President Franklin Roosevelt in his 1936 *General Theory of Employment, Interest and Money* . It wasn't until the implementation of Roosevelt's New Deal Reforms, based on the policy ideas of Keynes, followed by the economic expansion from World War II, that the U.S. economy got back on track. The debate as to whether an economy should be based on central state planning or decentralized market prices was in full swing.

World War II was a war caused, in part, by economics. The German disgust over the forced World War I reparations and the subsequent German hyperinflation enabled the rise to power of Adolf Hitler, who became Chancellor of Germany in 1934 with a nationalistic perspective combined with a belief that the Aryan race was superior to others.

Hitler's attack on Poland in 1939 thrust the world into World War II, in which France, Britain, Russia, China, and the United States (and their colonial-tied countries) fought Germany, Italy, and Japan (and the countries they influenced).

World War II brought destruction to lives, dignity, and property. From the Holocaust extermination camps in Germany and Poland to the Nanjing Massacre in China, humanity went through a six year period that showed the worst of the human condition.

Although three generations have now passed since those times, we hope we never forget the horrors of World War II. Continued innovation in global communication technologies and trade continues to bring us closer together as a single, empathic species in which we all see ourselves as part of the same human tribe. Happily, the internet is beginning to play a major role in creating a single connected human identity and consciousness at the species level, we believe reducing the likelihood of the breakout of full scale conflict.

While the original efforts at unification after World War I, *The League of Nations*, did not pan out, by June 1945, the United Nations was created by 51 original signatories. The UN was designed to reduce conflict and provide a forum for diplomacy to reduce the likelihood of another devastating war.

A Forty Year Debate Over Markets

Churchill, Truman, and Stalin, allies at the end of World War II, wouldn't stay allies for long

In Britain, Clement Attlee won the 1945 election, defeating Winston Churchill. Atlee argued that the way forward was with a socialist state, with many private owners compelled to sell their businesses to the State. The British government took over enterprises like coal, steel, and the railroads. The sense was that the best path to development was through government ownership of the largest, most important industries.

In Germany, because of the separation between East and West Berlin, there was a unique opportunity to see a comparison of the two competing economic models. Ludwig Erhard, from 1946 to 1949, was the West German Minister of Economics. One of Erhard's first tasks as Minister of Economics was slowing hyperinflation by removing price controls to enable markets to properly function and get goods into stores. In the following decades, West Germany would have a competitive market economic combined with a strong safety net.

In 1947, India became independent of Britain and Jawaharlal Nehru became the first Prime Minister. Nehru led India into an economic model focused on the scientific state planning of a mixed economy. India's socialist model was looked to across the developing world as the preferred model of development. By 1950, Socialism, planning, government control, and government ownership became the standard in the developing world. India chose to shut out foreign imports based on the ideals of self-sufficiency, a decision later reversed in the 1990s.

By the end of the 1940s, tensions grew as the dominant division was no longer between Democracy and Fascism, but between Capitalism and Communism. In 1949, Mao Zedong's Communist Party of China won the Chinese Civil War and set up the People's Republic of China, sending much of the formerly ruling nationalist party to Taiwan.

In 1950, the U.S. entered a war with the Soviets and China in Korea. Divided since 1945, the Korean Peninsula was split between a Soviet-backed government in the North and a Western-backed government in the South. Northern forces crossed the 38th parallel in June 1950 and had nearly consolidated the entirety of the Peninsula by late June 1950.

President Truman, backing up his Truman Doctrine that he would not let Communism spread, sent in American troops under General MacArthur to Korea, creating a drawn-out three year war with massive casualties and numerous massacres in which the USSR, China, and North Korea battled the

United States and South Korea. Over 500,000 troops were killed on both sides, with another 2.5 million civilians killed or wounded.[17]

To put into context just how active the proxy wars were between the USSR and the USA, here's a partial list the countries that had civil wars, coups, or revolutions related to the "Cold" War between communism and capitalism in the three decades between 1950 and 1980: North Korea (1950), Iran (1953), Guatemala (1954), Brazil (1964), Vietnam (1965), Greece (1967), Cambodia (1970), Bolivia (1971), Chile (1973), El Salvador (1979), and Afghanistan (1979).

The Soviet Union continued until 1991 when it became clear the experiment of a centrally planned economy had failed and the Union disbanded and modernized. It was too hard and inefficient to organize a market for millions of people and millions of goods without the distributed price signals of a market. Without competitive incentives to produce quality goods and a price signal that ensured needed goods were available in stores, hundreds of millions suffered.

A key turning point in Soviet Leader Boris Yeltsin's decision to dissolve the Soviet Union and move away from a centrally planned state came during a visit to a Texas grocery store in 1989 when he saw in front of him such a variety of foods available on the shelves and compared it to what he had seen in Moscow. Yeltsin was amazed that great selection and quality of what available in a standard American grocery store versus the grocery stores in Moscow.[18]

The 1980s-era combination of Ronald Reagan in the U.S. and Margaret Thatcher in the UK and the collapse of the Soviet Union led the pendulum to swing back toward a global belief in competitive market economies. In the 1980s and 1990s, industries around the world were privatized, regulations were reduced, and the model of the market-driven economy became the primary world model.

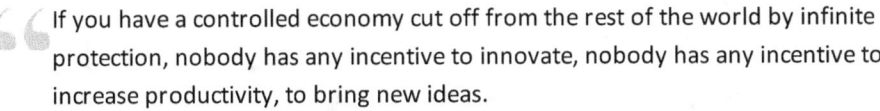

> If you have a controlled economy cut off from the rest of the world by infinite protection, nobody has any incentive to innovate, nobody has any incentive to increase productivity, to bring new ideas.
>
> - Manmohan Singh, Finance Minister, '91-'96, later the Prime Minister of India[19]

Recommended Chapter Resources:

Video: <u>The History of The World in Two Hours, The History Channel</u>

Book: <u>The Worldly Philosophers</u> by Robert Heilbroner

Video: <u>The Ascent of Money</u>, By Niall Ferguson

Part III. The Present

Ch 7. A Globalizing World

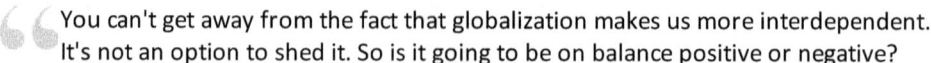 You can't get away from the fact that globalization makes us more interdependent. It's not an option to shed it. So is it going to be on balance positive or negative?

- Bill Clinton, 42nd President of the United States

The Globalized World

The Shanghai Skyline in 2009

Let's briefly look at how the global economic and financial system that we live in today was created.

Near the end of World War II, in 1944, the Allied powers gathered in Bretton Woods, New Hampshire, to lay out the rules of the new global economic system. The Bretton Woods conference created the World Bank and the International Monetary Fund, and laid the foundations for the 1947 General Agreement of Tariffs and Trade (GATT), the forerunner to the World Trade Organization and our global economic system.

The Bretton Woods delegates established these global organizations to govern international trade and finance in the hope of never returning to the protectionist economic policies that decreased trade, fostered an "us vs. them mentality," and worsened the Great Depression.

Economic globalization and interconnection did not come without event. The 1997 Asian crisis followed the Thai Baht devaluation, caused by markets overly open to speculative currency trades. The 1998 Argentinian default followed a similar track. In the 1999 Seattle meetings, the 2001 Doha meetings, and the 2003 Cancun meetings of the World Trade Organization, developing countries combined forces to negotiate updates to the rules to allow emerging markets to better participate in global progress.

In 1979 the World Economic Forum began publishing an annual Global Competitiveness Report and in 2004 the World Bank (based in Washington D.C.) began publishing an annual Doing Business Report comparing business regulations in 185 countries. The global drive toward trade, cooperation, and standardization of markets was on.

In the 2000s, the global trend toward social and environmental responsibility for business expanded as discussions about the role of business in taking care of customers, employees, and their communities expanded in reaction to the 2008 financial crisis and the growing concern over off-balance sheet externalities like carbon pollution. It became clear that companies who only focused on short-term maximization of cash flow were not becoming the long term winners. This "socially responsible capitalism" was fortunately far from the inefficient and destructive centrally controlled and planned markets of the mid 20th century--yet still had much reform ahead.

Population Grows as Prosperity Expands

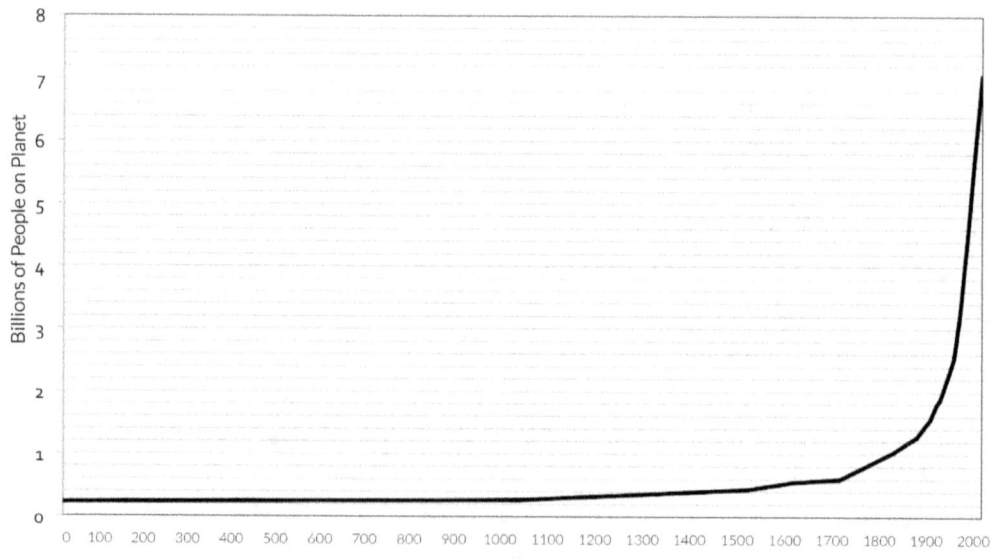

World Population has grown from 1 billion to over 7 billion in the last 200 years

In the 19th century, human population grew 60% from 1.0 billion to 1.6 billion.

Then, in the 20th century, human population skyrocketed nearly 300% from 1.6 billion to 6.1 billion. Today, population has passed 7.2 billion and is expected to reach 9 billion by 2050. Through progress in medicine, markets, machines, and food production this immense population growth been possible over the last two hundred years.

With greater population, of course, comes the ability for scientists to finally have the economic incentive to solve rare diseases and the ability for economies of scale to enable complex supply chains that bring every good to your local markets, greatly expanding choice.

While some have lamented population growth, more human beings being able to survive and live longer lives is a *result* of progress, not a hindrance to progress.

> O, wonder! How many goodly creatures are there here! How beauteous mankind is! O brave new world, That has such people in't!
>
> —William Shakespeare, *The Tempest*

The "Green Revolution" in agriculture of the 1970s and 80s, spurred on by Nobel Peace Prize winner Norman Borlaug, enabled billions to be spared from the ravages of starvation hunger. Higher-yield seeds combined with the expanded use of fertilizers proved many wrong who wondered whether population would again plateau.

There have been two enablers of the immense population growth we've seen in the last two centuries a) the invention of the engine and ability to replace human muscle with automated machinery and b) the great advances in agricultural science and production around the world.

From these two advances came an unprecedented ability to support over 7 billion people. We don't yet live in a world in which all of us have enough--but this world is coming and directly ahead.

After a 20th century of warfare, conflict, and a battle of ideas between centrally planned and market economies, the global system is finally moving toward greater global stability, transparency, and rules that make it easier for anyone to start and build a business and solve problems in their community or around the world. That said, this system still has a long way to go to be fair to all participants and be truly structured in a way that fit the principles of justice from Chapter One.

Recommended Chapter Resources:

Video: *The Commanding Heights* by PBS (Part 1) (Part 2) (Part 3)

Report: The WEF Global Competitiveness Report

Ch 8. The Magical Information Age

" Over two billion people now use the broadband Internet, up from perhaps 50 million a decade ago, when I was at Netscape, the company I co-founded. In the next 10 years, I expect at least five billion people worldwide to own smartphones, giving every individual with such a phone instant access to the full power of the Internet, every moment of every day... The result is a global economy that for the first time will be fully digitally wired—the dream of every cyber-visionary of the early 1990s, finally delivered, a full generation later.

- Marc Andreessen, "Why Software is Eating the World"

A 26 Year Old Starts a Transformation

The Z1, the world's first programmable computer, created in 1938

That smartphone you have in your pocket? Well, it wouldn't be there if Konrad Zuse hadn't been just a little bit crazy.

It was 1936, and 26 year old Konrad Zuse was hunched over, working in the bathroom of his parents' apartment in Berlin, Germany. He had just quit his stable job in airplane construction at Henschel Aviation.

Zuse was frustrated by the many routine calculations he had to make by hand in his job as a civil engineer. He knew these calculations could be done by a machine.[20]

So he quit to build the world's first programmable computer, building upon the earlier work of Charles Babbage's analytical engine and James Thomas' differential analyzer. Working mostly alone, Zuse finished the Z1 in 1938.

Konrad Zuse and the many who followed him in the 1940s and 1950s building the first programmable computers were the early pioneers of the Information Age.

Encoding Into Bits

In the Industrial Age, work was done through the mechanical effort of engines, powered by steam, water, petroleum, and electricity. In the Information Age, much that was previously physical or analog could be turned into binary bits -- encoded pieces of information processed by microprocessors.

Here are a few examples.

	Industrial Age 1712-1950	Information Age 1950-2015
Calculating	Hand Calculations	Digital Calculator
Telling Time	Mechanical clock	Digital Watch
Writing	Pen and paper	Word Processor
Publishing	Printing press	Save to the cloud
Designing	Pen and paper	Design Software
Creating Objects	Mold creation	3D Printing
Navigating	Compass	GPS App
Health Records	Manilla folders	Digital Software
Animation	Hand drawn	Digital Software
Buying Stocks	Broker on Trading Floor	Digital Software
Encyclopedia	Controlled Books	Digital Hive Mind

We start the Information Age in 1950 due to Bill Shockley's 1947 invention of the transistor, a device used to amplify and switch electronic signals, and the 1949 creation of the first commercially-available computer, the UNIVAC.

It would however take until the invention of the early internet in 1969, the microprocessor in 1971, and the first personal computer in 1972 for the Information Age to begin to spread globally. These three inventions enabled the mass utilization of computers.

Once a process can be turned from physical into digital, tremendous innovation and cost reduction follows. To convert a process from physical in nature to information in nature, one key step is to convert inputs and outputs into binary format. The binary system was invented in 1649 by a German mathematician named Gottfried Leibniz.

Binary format enables the storing of information with less hard drive space, which was initially quite hard to come by, as the possibilities are simply 0 (meaning "off") or 1 (meaning "on").

Here are few examples of converting binary numbers to regular numbers.

$001 = 2^0 = 1$

$$010 = 2^1 = 2$$
$$100 = 2^2 = 4$$

Here are a couple more examples.

3 in binary format is 11.
This is because $1*2^1 + 1*2^0 = 3$.

25 in binary format is 11001.
This is because $1*2^4 + 1*2^3 + 0*2^2 + 0*2^1 + 1*2^0 = 25$.

To a computer, the number 25 is simply "on, on, off, off, on." Imagine talking like that!

Computer programming languages are simply ways of taking standard expressions that human programmers can understand like:

Print("Hello World!")

And turning that input into the machine code of 1s and 0s for the computer to execute the command, then turning the output back into the alphanumeric languages humans understand. Thus, roughly speaking

Print("3+6") becomes in binary: 11 + 110

The computer then executes that binary instruction to come up with:
11 + 110 = 1001

And translates back from binary to numeric to display the answer.
$1*2^3 + 0*2^2 + 0*2^1 + 1*2^0 = 9$

In a fiber optic cable 1001, this would look something like:
Light, No Light, No Light, Light = 1001 = 9

While this system sounds complicated, to a computer it's much more efficient to only have to remember a logic system that is based on on and off.

Back in 1995, Harvard Business School professor Clayton Christensen coined the term "disruptive technologies" that turned into his 1997 book "The Innovator's Dilemma"

Today, the reason why software is disrupting the world is that decades of manual physical processes are being turned into automated and easy binary and digital processes.

> Software is eating the world. More and more major businesses and industries are being run on software and delivered as online services—from movies to agriculture to national defense. Many of the winners are Silicon Valley-style entrepreneurial technology companies that are invading and overturning established industry structures. Over the next 10 years, I expect many more industries to be disrupted by software, with new world-beating Silicon Valley companies doing the disruption in more cases than not.
>
> - Marc Andreessen, "Why Software is Eating the World"

We wonder what will be next on this list of innovations? Will you be part of a team that creates of the most important innovations in human history? Here is how Singularity University, an organization dedicated to applying exponential technologies to solve humanity's greatest challenges, summarizes the last 10,000 years of human history.

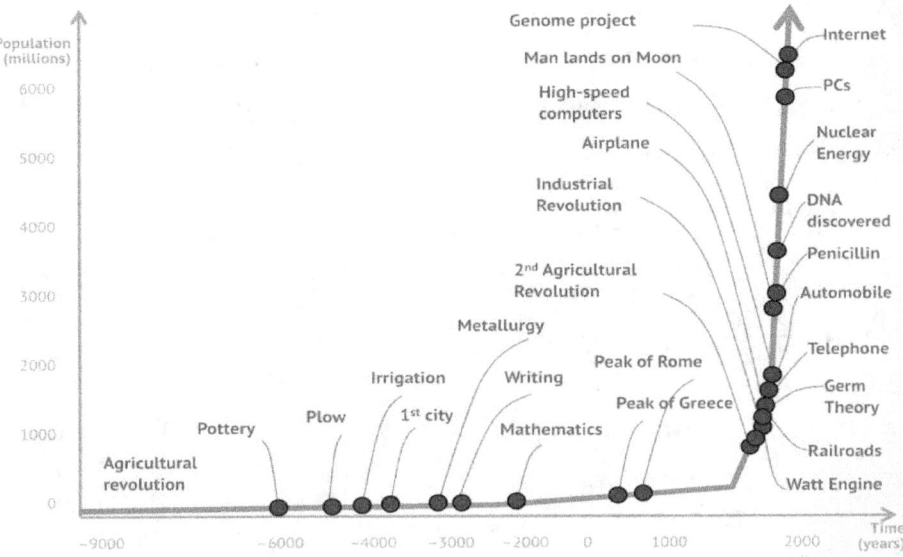

Timeline of Information Age Innovation

DNA (1953) – In 1953, James Watson and Francis Crick discovered DNA while working at Cambridge University. The duo suggested that the correct model for DNA structure was the double helix model and famously walked into a local pub and exclaimed, "We have found the secret of life."

The Integrated Circuit (1959)- In 1959, we saw the creation and discovery of the integrated circuit. Integrated circuits allow engineers to fit a lot more transistors, resistors, and capacitors in a smaller area. It was Jack Kilby of Texas Instruments and Robert Noyce of Fairchild Semiconductor, along with their teams, who created the first integrated circuits in 1959. All computers eventually ended up using integrated circuits, which later developed into microprocessors.

The Internet (1969) – In 1969, we saw the creation of the early Internet, called the ARPANET, which was built by the United States Department of Defense Advanced Research Projects Agency (then called ARPA, today called DARPA) to connect researchers at different locations. The ARPANET delivered its first message on October 29, 1969 between UCLA and Stanford. The first message was simply the word "log in." The message crashed the network and only the first two letters, L and O, made it through. By the end of 1969, four computers were connected to the ARPANET.

Microprocessors (1971) – In 1971, Ted Hoff of Intel created the microprocessor, which was an integrated circuit. It had all the functions of the computer or a central processing unit (CPU) on it, in a tiny space. The first chip was called the Intel 4004. It had 2300 transistors on it. It had as much power in one single chip as the ENIAC supercomputer, a 30-ton computer built in 1946. The microprocessor led to the miniaturization and the creation of the PC industry in the late 1970s, 1980s, and 1990s, which enables us to have a supercomputer in our pockets today, connected to the global Internet–an amazingly important invention in human history that happened only a little more than four decades ago.

The Mobile Phone (1973) – In 1973, Motorola launched the first handheld mobile phone. The first prototype weighed 2.5 pounds, offered 30 minutes of talk time, and featured a battery that took ten hours to recharge.

The World Wide Web (1991) - It took until 1991 for the creation of the Hypertext Transfer Protocol (HTTP) by Tim Berners-Lee, which enabled the creation of a web of hyperlink documents. The World Wide Web became a communication tool that formed a constantly updating record of human knowledge and expression. A year later, in 1992, researchers of the University of Illinois developed a browser that created a user-friendly way to view the World Wide Web. Initially called Mosaic, that first browser turned into the company and product Netscape, which revolutionized the ability of individuals to access information globally.

The Smartphone (2007) – On January 9, 2007, the iPhone launched, the first widely available smartphone with multi-touch capabilities. The lowly telephone had turned into a cloud-connected smartphone with built-in GPS, compass, voice recorder, camera, maps, and web browser with an app store that allowed the user to download from a selection of millions of specialty applications. The multitouch smartphone paved the way for the tablet and the coming convergence of the laptop/tablet/and smartphone and new hybrids such as cloud-connected glasses and smartwatches. A world with smartphones with sufficient processing power and memory to be used as full-featured computers connected via docking stations to flexible frame monitors with hand gesture inputs and a projected keypad was soon approaching.

The Quantum Computer (2011) – The last step in our brief history of innovation is the quantum computer. In 2011, the first quantum computer was brought to market by D-wave. It was called the D-wave One. Quantum computers use superposition and entanglement to solve some computing problems thousands of times faster than traditional computers. In May 2013 Google announced it was purchasing a D-wave Two quantum computer to be hosted at the Quantum Artificial Research Lab at the NASA Ames Research Center in Mountain View, CA.

Ch 9. The Parental Report Card

> If somehow we could be given a pill to be convinced that all would turn out okay, would that elicit from us our greatest creativity and courage? No. It is that knife-edge of uncertainty when we come alive to our greatest power.
>
> —Joanna Macy, environmentalist

Measuring Human Progress

The inner cover illustration of the 1772 Encyclopédie by Denis Diderot. The figure in the center represents truth and is surrounded by bright light, the central symbol of the 18th Century Enlightenment.

In this chapter, we'll look at the global trends on health, income, education, peace, and the environment--to see whether this new system was creating better or worse results for humanity.

Let's start, by comparing 1900 with 2012 across five key measures:

	1900	2012
1. Life Expectancy	32[21]	70[22]
2. Infant Mortality	19.5%[23]	3.69%[24]
3. Per Person Income	$2000[25]	$10,395[26]
4. % In Extreme Poverty	68.7%[27]	16.9%[28]
5. Literacy Rate	42%[29]	84%[30]

Since the beginning of the 20th century, global life expectancy has increased by 118%, infant mortality has declined by 81%, per person income has improved by 403% (in real dollars), all while human population has increased by more than 4x from 1.7 billion to 7.1 billion.

As a species, we've made immense progress over the last century. We've made this progress during a period in which we saw the Green Revolution in agricultural productivity, the invention of personal computing, and the creation of the internet.

> Suppose that you stuffed me and my family into a time machine, sent us back a century to 1890... I would want, first, health insurance: the ability to go to the doctor and be treated with late-twentieth-century medicines. Franklin Delano Roosevelt was crippled by polio. Without antibiotic and adrenaline shots I would now be dead of childhood pneumonia. The second thing I would want would be utility hookups--electricity and gas, central heating, and consumer appliances. The third thing I want to buy is access to information--audio and video broadcasts, recorded music, computing power, and access to databases. None of these were available *at any price* back in 1890.
>
> —Brad DeLong, *Slouching Toward Utopia, The Economic History of the 20th Century*

In 1798 Thomas Malthus made a famous prediction in *An Essay on the Principle of Population* that world population would level off due to famine. At the time the population was just under 1 billion people.

Unfortunately for Malthus, he didn't properly take into account the impact of the Industrial revolution and the agricultural revolution in expanding the food production capabilities of the 19th and 20th centuries and advancements in medical science (like penicillin) greatly expanding our life expectancy.

News publishers know that the human brain is instinctually structured to pay more attention to bad news and danger. Our brain's amygdala developed on the grasslands of Eastern Africa 50,000 years ago to ensure that information connected to possible danger was processed and remembered with much higher priority than information connected to opportunity and safety.

The early homo sapiens who paid attention to and remembered danger were those who prosperous and reproduced, creating an evolutionary selection for those with amygdalas that easily recalled danger. Peter Diamandis writes about this principle extensively in his 2012 book *Abundance.*

Often those predicting doom are either doing it for the sake of selling news or are doing it because they aren't factoring into their models how rapidly the combination of the market system, specialization, and investments in technology are creating solutions to the major challenges facing humanity.

Creating A Parental Report Card

But are we doing better or worse as a species than a generation ago in 1980? Are things generally getting better or getting worse? Let's develop a report card for our parents ("Baby Boomers" born between 1940 and 1960 for the most part) and see how they have stewarded our society and species as they've been in leadership over the past few decades.

First, let's take a look at other measures of human progress. There are handful of existing ways to track human progress, including:

1. **The United Nations Human Development Index** - Created by the United Nations in 1990. It measures progress using three key measures: years of schooling, life expectancy, and gross national income. Ranks 187 countries.

2. **The Legatum Prosperity Index** - Started by the Legatum think tank based in Dubai. Ranks 142 countries.

3. **The Social Progress Index (SPI)** - Started by HBS professor Michael Porter and launched in 2013 at the Skoll World Forum for Social Enterprise in Oxford, England. Ranks 50 countries.

The limitation with these indices is that they measure on a country level rather than a species level. We could figure out if Lichtenstein is doing better than

Sweden with the above indices, but that's not our question. What we want to know is whether we're doing better or worse as a species than in 1980.

So, over the past few years, we've developed our own method for tracking human progress using global data from the World Bank, United Nations, and NASA that is available from 1980-2012.

We wanted to make sure our measure was comprehensive, so we selected the following five broad categories to gather data within.

1. Health
2. Education
3. Peace
4. Income
5. Environment

Within each of these five categories, we looked at two measures for the 32 year time period between 1980 and 2012. We looked at the following ten metrics to attempt to track overall human progress.

Ten Metrics to Track Human Progress	
Health	1. Life Expectancy 2. Infant Mortality
Education	3. Literacy 4. Internet Access
Peace	5. Active Conflicts 6. Deaths From War
Economics	7. Average Income 8. Global Poverty Rate
Environment	9. CO2 PPM 10. Temperature Increase

Let's look at each of the ten measures we selected, starting with health.

The Progress on Health

First, we looked at Global Life Expectancy from 1980 to 2012. We felt that how long people live on average is a good proxy for global health. In just three decades, life expectancy of people around the world went up by 12%.

1. Life Expectancy

1980
63 ⇒
2012
71

12% Higher

1982 1984 1986 1988 1990 1992 1994 1996 1998 2000 2002 2004 2006 2008 2011

Source: World Bank

Next we looked at infant mortality. Infant mortality occurs when a child dies before he or she reaches the age of five. Infant mortality decreased by 59% from 1981 to 2012. We smiled when we saw this. We were surprised at how much progress humanity has made in just one generation. Overall, the world has made great progress in our lifetime on human health.

2. Infant Mortality

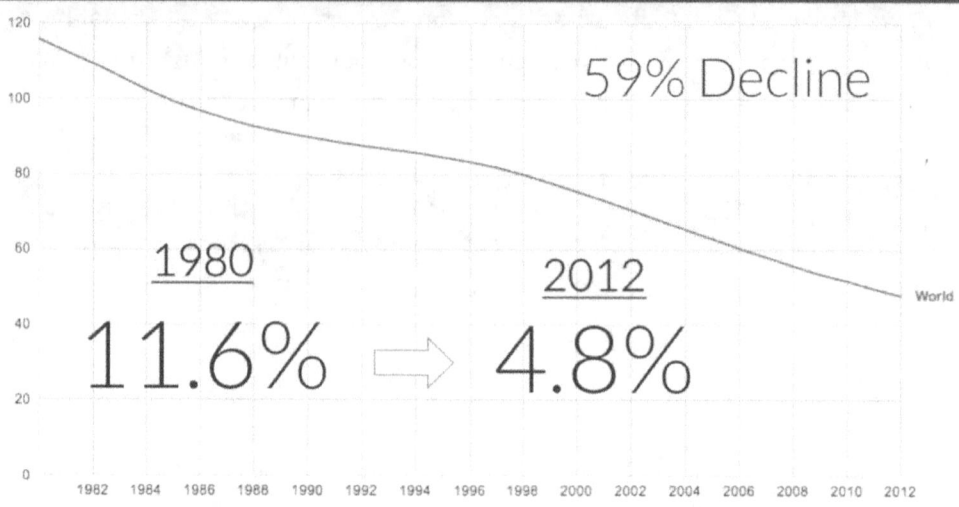

59% Decline

1980

2012

11.6% ⟹ 4.8%

World

Source: World Bank

The Progress on Education

Next, we looked up the data on education. We came across data from the World Bank on literacy. The World Bank defines literacy as "the ability to read and write a simple statement about your everyday life."

We started thinking just how grateful we are that we learned how to read and write early in life, and started thinking how difficult life would be if we were illiterate. When we look at the data, we saw from 1980 to 2012 the literacy rate of individuals age 15 and up increased from 70% to 84%.

3. Literacy Rate

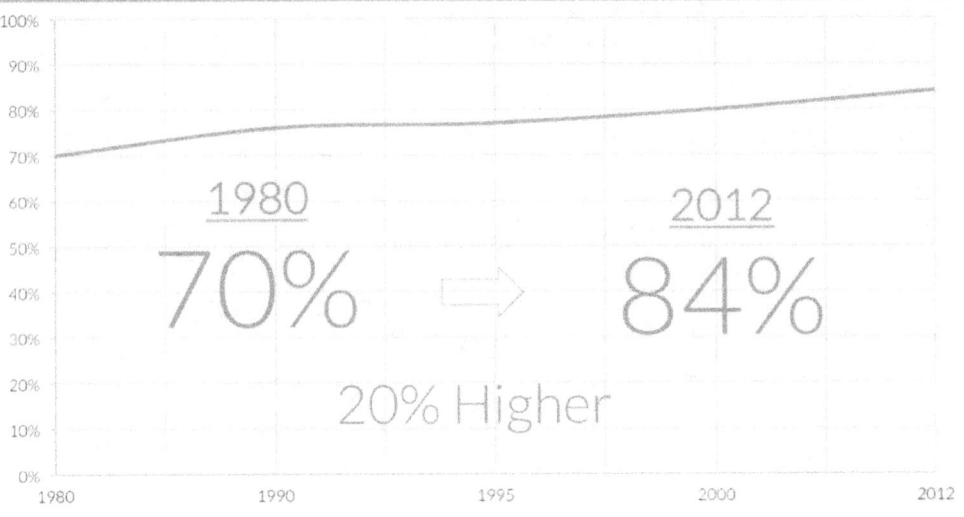

Source: World Bank

Since the mid-19th century, global adult literacy rates have greatly improved, from an estimated 10% in 1850 to 84% today in 2013. Ensuring that all people can read and write should also be a primary goal of every developing country's leader. Without the ability to read or write, you cannot fill out a job application or participate in the global economy.

Here's what UNESCO has to say about the progress we've made over the last 150 years.

 In the mid-nineteenth century, only 10% of the world's adult population could read or write. At the dawn of the twenty-first century, UNESCO estimates that over 80% of adults worldwide can read and write at some minimum level. This unprecedented social transformation occurred despite the world's population quintupling from about 1.2 billion in 1850 to over 6.4 billion [by 2006]... Literacy today, in its many manifestations, has become a vital set of competencies and practices, interwoven in the fabric of contemporary societies

- UNESCO Education for All Monitoring Report

As we began to think about the Internet, we realized we use it nearly everyday to communicate with our friends and family and often use sites like Wikipedia,

Khan Academy, EDx, Coursera, and Skillshare to learn. We realized just how important having access to an internet-connected mobile phone is to our lives.

When we looked at the data, we saw that in 2014, only 40% of the world had access to the internet. We wondered what you can do to ensure every person has access to the internet within the next decade or two, and started looking into the efforts of Internet.org, the Facebook Connectivity Lab, and Google to enable all people to access the internet.

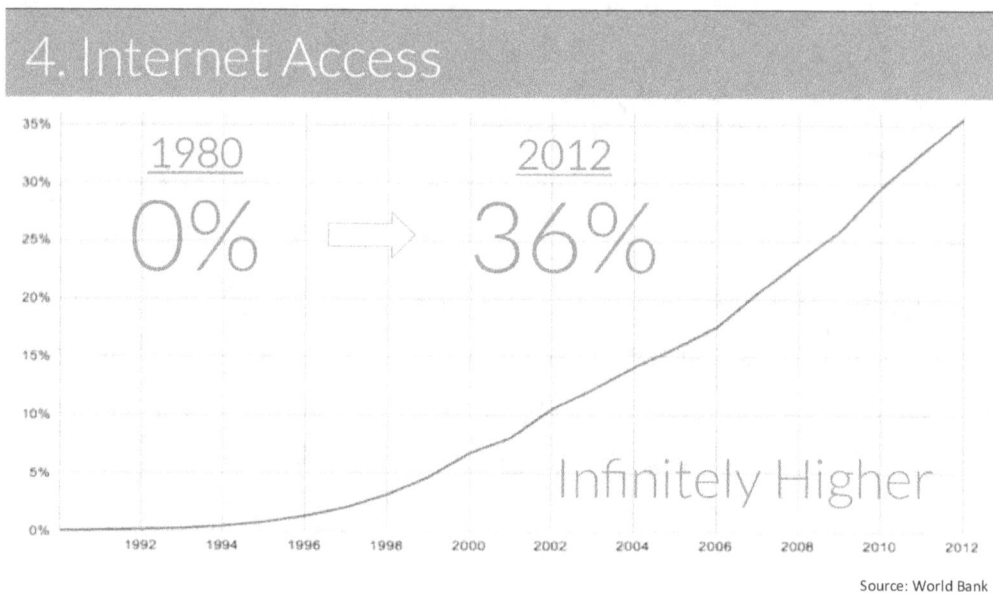

Source: World Bank

The Progress on Peace

Next up is global peace. We are enjoying the global perspective preparing these graphs is giving us.

To evaluate whether war is getting better or worse, we decided to look at both the number of global conflicts as well as how many people die per year in global conflicts.

We learned that the Uppsala Conflict Data Program has the most comprehensive records of global conflict going back to 1946. Uppsala defines a "major conflict" as any conflict that causes more than 1000 deaths per year.

We learned about the six recent conflicts in Iraq, Afghanistan, Syria, Northwest Mexico, the Congo, and Somalia. We were glad to see that the five year average has gone down a lot since the late 1980s and early 1990s when the Cold War was ending.

5. Active Global Conflicts

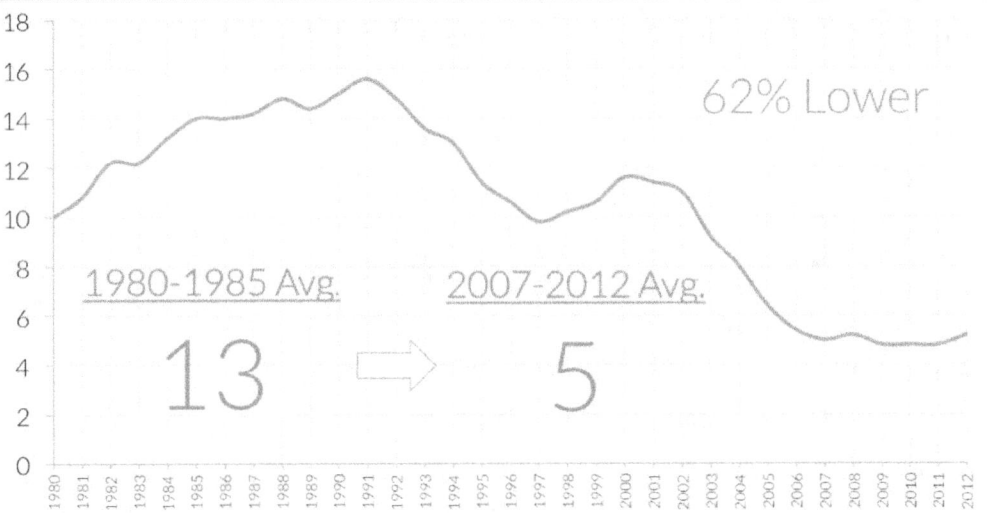

Source: Uppsala Conflict Data Program

Next, we looked at how many deaths per year occur from war.

We saw that the number of deaths from war have declined 41% since the early 1980s. We're impressed that in a time period when the population of the Earth grew from 4.4 billion to 7.0 billion both the number of wars and deaths from wars decreased substantially.

Still, 24,000 people dying every year from wars leaves a lot of room for improvement. We hope that within our lifetimes together we can create a world in which we all see each other as human beings who are part of the same global tribe and on the same team.

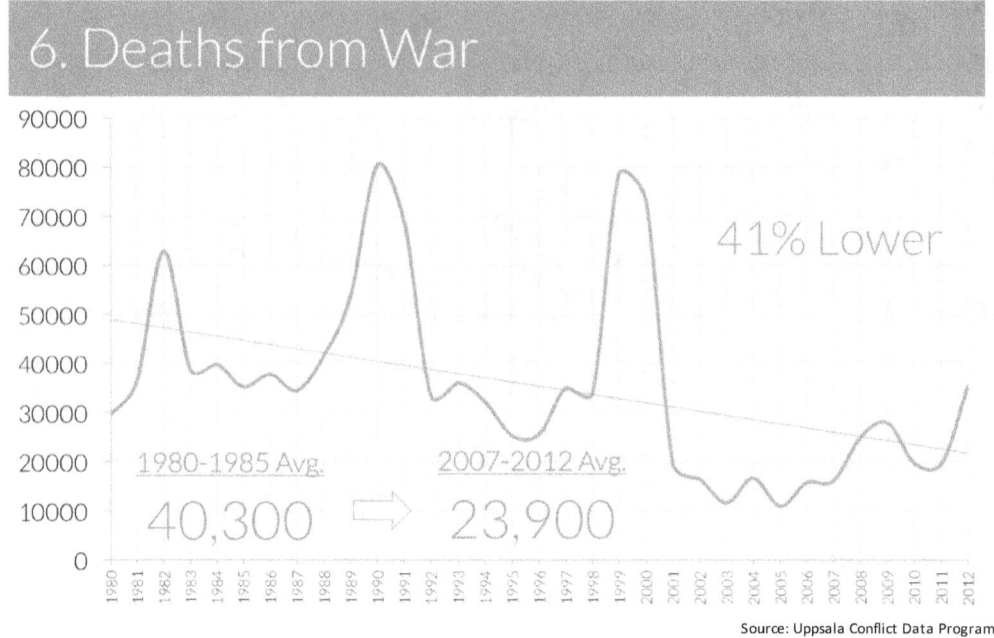

6. Deaths from War

41% Lower

1980-1985 Avg.
40,300 ⇨ 2007-2012 Avg.
23,900

Source: Uppsala Conflict Data Program

In his 2011 book, *The Better Angels of our Nature*, Harvard professor Steven Pinker makes the case that we may be living in the most peaceful time in human history, at least since the advent of agriculture and the beginnings of more densely populated civilizations 12,000 years ago.

After a tumultuous 20th century which saw events like WWI, WWII, the Holocaust, the Sino-Japanese war, the Korean War, Mao's Great Leap Forward, the Vietnam war, the Cambodian Genocide, the Gulf War, the Bosnian War, and the Rwandan genocide, it seems that over the last quarter century since the fall of the USSR and the beginning of the widespread use of the Internet we've entered a time of substantially less deadly conflict between and within nations.

The Progress on Economics

We began looking up data on global economics and thought about the simple question, "has the welfare of the average person gotten better or worse recently?" We decided to look at both the income of the average person as well as the percentage of people globally who live in extreme poverty.

We took a look at the average annual income statistics, and made doubly sure that they were in fact inflation adjusted. It turns out, the income of the average person in the world, in constant 2005 dollars, increased from $5960 in 1980 to $10,395 in 2012.

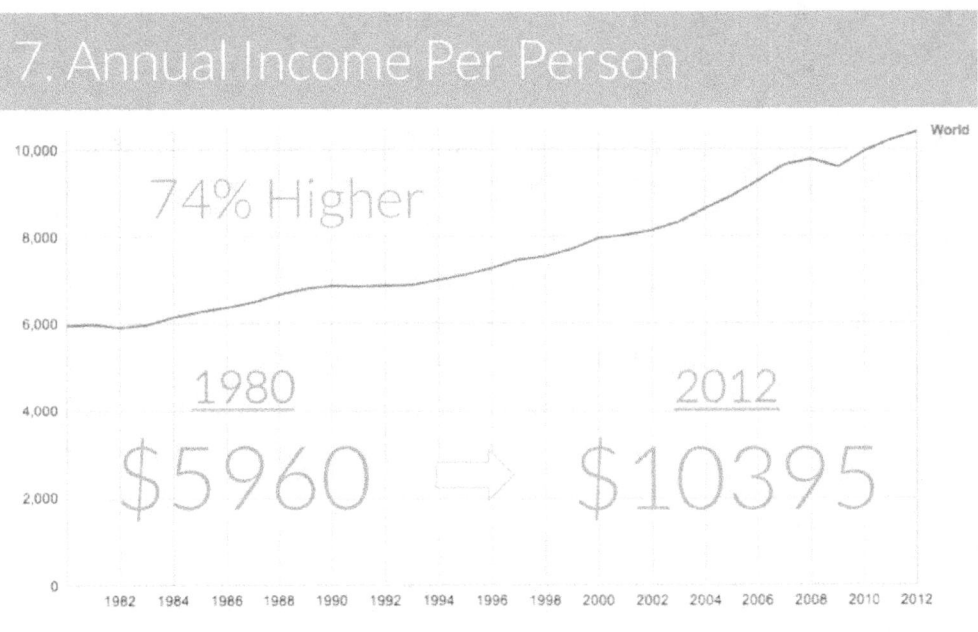

Source: World Bank

While we were excited that average income increased so much, we were most worried about poverty. We thought, "It doesn't really matter if average incomes are going up if there's more poverty than ever before." So we took a look at the data to see the trend.

We learned that the World Bank defines extreme poverty has "living on under $1.25 per day." If you earn above $1.25 per day (about $450 per year) then you have just enough to survive.

> Poverty's scourge is fiercest below $1.25: people below that level live lives that are poor, nasty, brutish and short. They lack not just education, health care, proper clothing and shelter—which most people in most of the world take for granted—but even enough food for physical and mental health. Raising people above that level of wretchedness is not a sufficient ambition for a prosperous planet, but it is a necessary one. The world's achievement in the field of poverty reduction is, by almost any measure, impressive.
>
> - The Economist, June 1, 2013

Below $1.25 per day and you barely have enough to survive. We couldn't imagine living on so little. We think about the fact that we often pay $3 for a coffee and $6 for a sandwich. It's hard to imagine paying for food and shelter and everything else with just $1.25 per day.

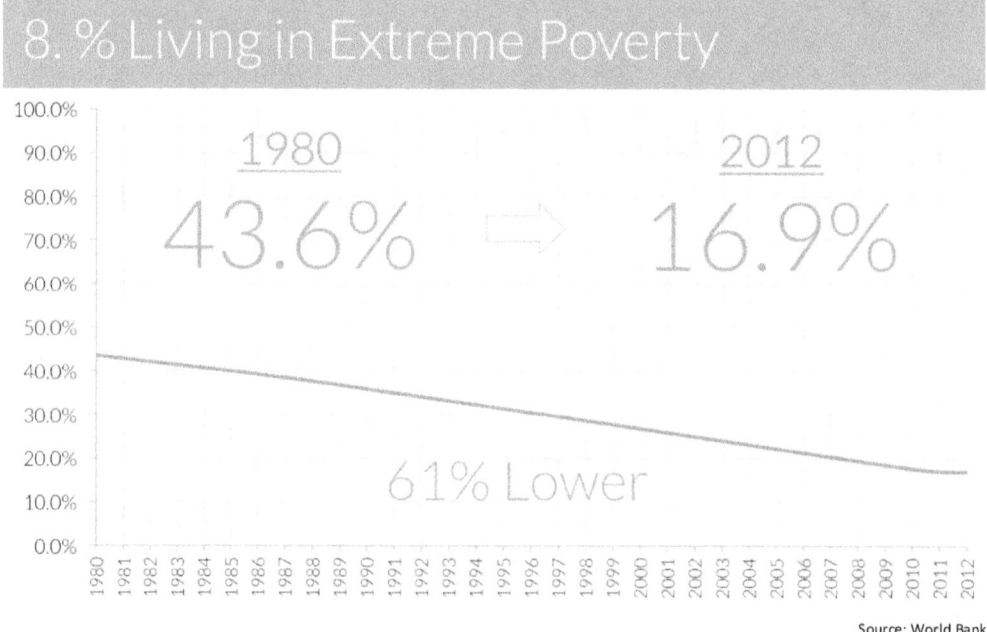

Source: World Bank

Back in 1980, 1.9 billion people lived in extreme poverty. By 2012, 1.2 billion people lived in extreme poverty globally. While over one billion people living in extreme poverty is still way too much, we were heartened to see the major progress that had been made.

Both the number and percentage of people living in extreme poverty today is much less than in 1980. So much has changed in just one generation with advances in science and global trade and the introduction of personal computers, software, the internet, and mobile phones.

> By 2025, the majority of the world's population will, in one generation, have gone from having virtually no access to unfiltered information to accessing all of the world's information through a device that fits in the palm of the hand.
>
> —Eric Schmidt and Jared Cohen, *The New Digital Age*

The Lack of Progress on the Environment

So far, we've been pleased to see major progress on health, education, peace, and economics. Now, we started looking at the metrics for the last category, the environment. Knowing about the dangers carbon dioxide (CO_2) poses to the continued ability of humans to live on Earth, we decided on the two environmental metrics to be the amount of CO_2 in the atmosphere and the increase in global temperatures.

Since 1980, the amount of carbon dioxide in the atmosphere increased by 19%. This figure is measured daily in Hawaii at the Mauna Loa Observatory. The more CO_2 there is in the atmosphere, the more the atmosphere traps heat, making the surface temperature on Earth warmer.

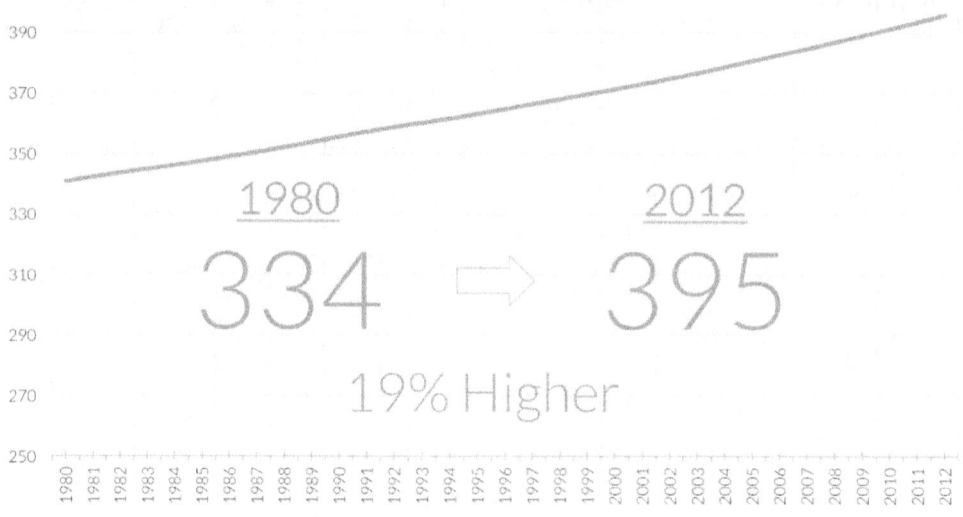

Source: NOAA

Next, we looked at how the temperature of the Earth increased since 1980. NASA's Goddard Institute for Space Studies keeps track of surface temperature changes each month with thousands of monitors all over the world. Back in 1980, they established a 30 year average baseline based on temperatures from 1951-1980. In 1980, the average global temperature was 0.61°F above the average. By 2012, the average global temperature was 1.37°F above the average, an increase of 125% in just 32 years.

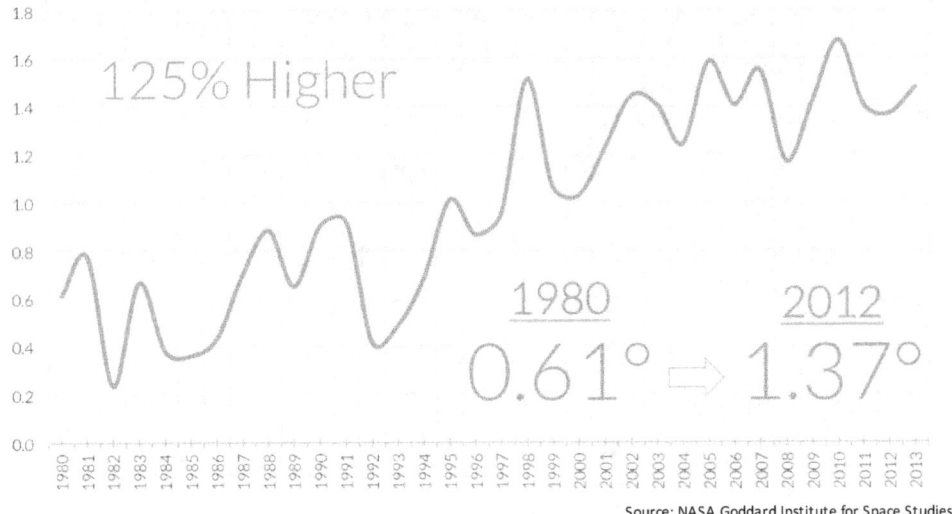

Source: NASA Goddard Institute for Space Studies

What concerns us most was that temperatures are on track to rise another 3°F to 7°F in the 21st century if we continue on our current path of getting most of the world's energy from fossil fuels, causing sea levels to rise, changing agricultural production zones, and increasing intensity of hurricanes and typhoons.

Knowing this, we realize just how important it is for us to move to a clean energy economy over the next couple decades.

Unless we make pretty rapid changes to a clean energy economy and away from fossil fuels over the next 20 years, we risk all of the progress we've made since 1900.

> The juggernaut of technology-based capitalism will not be stopped. It's momentum is reinforced by the billions of poor people in developing countries anxious to participate in order to share the material wealth of the industrialized nations. But its direction can be changed by mandate of a generally shared long-term environmental ethic. The choice is clear: the juggernaut will very soon either chew up what remains of the living world, or it will be redirected to save it.

The earth's environment is not an issue delinked from human progress. The Earth is the place on which nearly all human progress has taken place. As the noted biologist E.O. Wilson says, "...the planet... is a little sphere with a razor-thin coat of life too fragile to bear careless tampering."

Yet even E.O. Wilson himself sees technology, science, and human progress as part of the solution to a sustainable future, not as part of the problem. He says in *The Future of Life* (2002), "Science and technology also promise the means for raising per-capita food production while decreasing materials and energy consumption, both of which are preconditions for successful long-term conservation and a sustainable economy."

Perhaps, then, it is the discovery of petroleum in 1859 in Edward Drake's steam engine well in Pennsylvania that has in part led to humanity having such high-standards of living today--standards of living that for once allow us to afford to invest in creating a carbon neutral world by 2040 that is prosperous for all of us, unlike the low carbon and low living-standard world of 1840 that was brutish, difficult, and short, with low literacy rates, a lack of sanitation, no electricity or sewage removal, and high infant mortality.

Historically, fossil fuels have been a great thing for humanity. Now that we know that the continued use of fossil fuels will threaten the progress they have so far enabled, we must use our wealth and scientific energy to move toward clean energy as quickly as possible.

Our Parents' Report Card

Finally, we brought all the metrics together into one "Global Report Card" for our parents.

The Global Report Card		1980	2012	% Change	Grade
Health	1. Life Expectancy	63	71	⇧ 12%	A
	2. Infant Mortality	11.6%	4.8%	⇩ 59%	A
Education	3. Literacy	70%	84%	⇧ 20%	B
	4. Internet Access	0%	36%	⇧ Infinite	B
Peace	5. Active Conflicts	13	5	⇩ 62%	B
	6. Deaths from War	40,300	23,900	⇩ 41%	B
Economics	7. Average Income	$5.9k	$10.4k	⇧ 74%	A
	8. Poverty Rate	43.6%	16.9%	⇩ 61%	B
Environment	9. CO2 PPM	334	395	⇧ 19%	F
	10. Temp. Increase	+0.61°	+1.37°	⇧ 125%	F

We took one final look at the metrics we chose. We realized one is missing...
happiness. We did some research and realized that global data on human
happiness began being collected in 156 countries starting in 2005 by the
creators of the World Happiness Report from Columbia University, the London
School of Economics, and the University of British Columbia.

As our global standards of living increase, watching what happens to our
happiness levels will be important. A 2010 study by Princeton researchers
Daniel Kahneman and Angus Deaton, showed that emotional well-being does
correlate with increases in income up to $75,000, but did not rise further after
reaching $75,000.[32]

We look forward to including happiness as a measure in our next Global Report
Card.

After millennia of only gradual improvements in living standards, it's stunning
to observe what happened to both human population and standards of living
between 1800 and 2012 as we made rapid advances in food production,
sanitation, healthcare, and economic models. Below is a chart showing the per

person income (in 2005 dollars) in gray graphed against the increase in billions of people on the planet in black.

The early 21st century is the best time in human history to be alive. Life expectancy, per capita income, and literacy rates are the highest in human history, medicine is the most advanced it has ever been, the cost of starting a new company is lower than ever before, and the size of global market makes almost any niche able to achieve economies of scale.

Now, in our generation we have the opportunity to create a world that works for everybody. A world in which every person has access to their basic needs of food, water, shelter, education, and medicine. A world that is sustainable. And a world that is joyous.

Whenever you read a news article that leaves you feeling down about the world, come back to this chart below showing the global population rising and per capita income rising right along with it. Pay special attention to the immense progress we've made in over the last 200 years and the last generation.

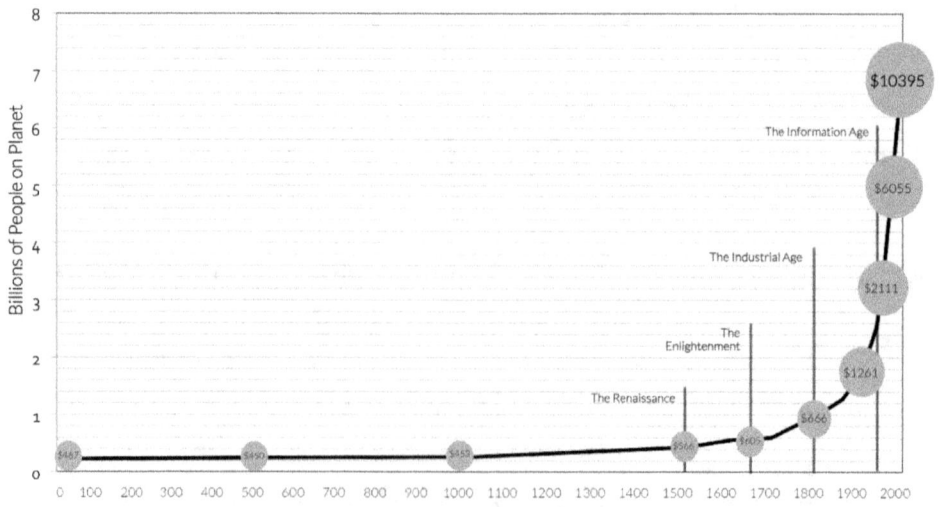

Recommended Chapter Resources:

- Book: _Abundance_ by Peter Diamandis
- Book: _The Rational Optimist_ by Matt Ridley
- Book: _The Better Angels of Our Nature_ by Steven Pinker
- Book: _Getting Better_ by Charles Kenny
- Book: _The Future of Life_ by E.O. Wilson
- Book: _Sex At Dawn_ (Chapters 11-14) by Christopher Ryan and Cacilda Jetha
- Video: _Understanding The Science for Tomorrow: Myth vs. Reality_ by Jeffrey Grossman
- Site: The Earth Dashboard

Part IV. The Future

Ch 10. Entering The Innovation Age

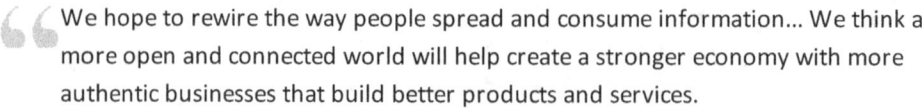 We hope to rewire the way people spread and consume information... We think a more open and connected world will help create a stronger economy with more authentic businesses that build better products and services.

—Mark Zuckerberg, CEO of Facebook, Letter to Potential Shareholders, May 2012

A Major Tipping Point

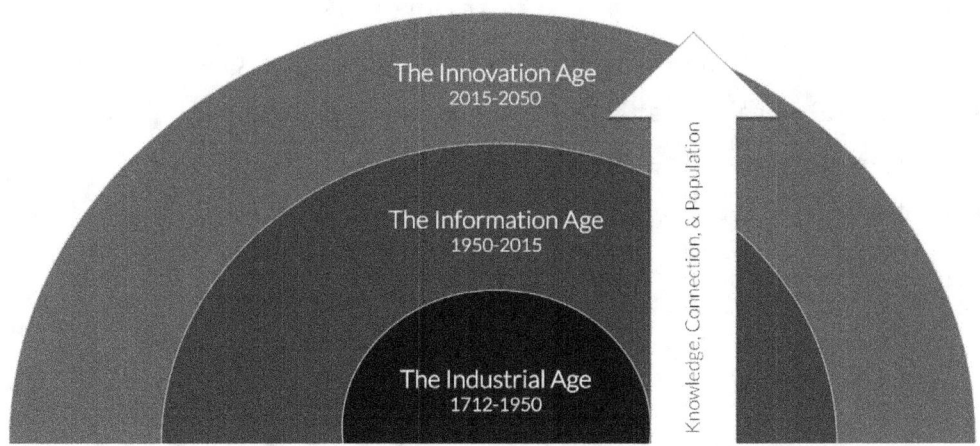

Now it is time to transition from understanding the past, to creating the future.

The Innovation Age will begin at the end of 2015 *when for the first time more than 50% of humans have access to the cloud*. As of 2014, 39% of humanity has internet access. That number will reach 50% by the end of 2015 in a major tipping point for our species. Instead of the lucky few having access to free cloud education, soon all humans will be able to benefit from sites like EDx, Wikipedia, and Khan Academy.

Humans have made great advances since 1800 as we've come through the Industrial Age (1712-1950) to the Information Age—enabling human population to grow from 1 billion to 7.2 billion in just two centuries.

The Information Age began with the advent of commercially available computers in 1950 and will end with the start of the Innovation Age. The Information Age has brought with it the greatest sixty-five years in the history of human progress, leading to substantial increases in life-expectancy, per capita income, and literacy and significant decreases in infant mortality and the number of people living in poverty around the world.

Now, as we enter the Innovation Age (2015-2050), we stand on the shoulders of giants who have come before us. Synthetic biology is here. Clean renewable energy is here. Global connection is here. The platforms have been built. We are now entering the most exciting time in human history for creators and innovators.

You'll notice that each subsequent "Age" in our diagram takes fewer years. The Industrial Age took 238 years, the Information Age 65 years, and The Innovation Age just 35 years. We expect that these epochs in history will indeed go faster due to the much greater access to knowledge and the many greater people in the world. Within the ecosystem of our species, the greater the distribution of knowledge and the greater the interconnection across cultures, the faster memes can replicate, learnings can be shared, and progress can be made.

The rate of progress is a function of the rate of ideas spreading, which itself is a function of the speed of communication and the depth and breadth of interconnection among our species.

$$Rate\ of\ Progress = f\ (Rate\ of\ Ideas\ Spreading)$$

$$Rate\ of\ Ideas\ Spreading = f\ (Speed\ of\ Communication\ Tools\ x\ Level\ of\ Species\ Interconnection)$$

And of course, the rate of ideas spreading across our species is faster than ever before due to rapid speeds of communication and a much greater depth and breadth of global interconnection than ever before. The rate of ideas spreading directly relates to the speed of cultural evolution. We've evolving as a species culturally faster than ever before in part due to the rapid high-fidelity communication tools that is spreading understanding and connection across borders faster than at any prior time in human history.

We are, in part, writing this book to spread the idea that it is up to our generation to put in place the policy and technological conditions for a sustainable and prosperous world.

The rate that the key memes in this book of "sustainable prosperity" and "species-level empathy" and "equality of opportunity" spread will be a function of the speed of the communication tools we use, the level of species interconnection, and of course the willingness of those hearing the idea to spread it to others.

Wonderfully, the speed of communication tools we are using, the level of species-wide literacy, and the level of species interconnection are all rapidly increasing, leading to rapid evolution of culture.

There is a palpable sense that the leaders of the Millennial Generation (such as Jared Cohen, Joshua Gorman, Andrew Mangino, Chelsea Clinton, Johnny Dorsey, Barbara Bush, Shiza Shahid, Malala Yousafzai, and Clemantine Wamariya among many others) see beyond the divisions of national borders and religious identities that have kept us as human beings apart for many centuries. This is a truly exciting time to live.

The Great Opportunity

Our next great opportunity is creating a carbon-neutral world in which every human has access to what they need to thrive. Prosperous sustainability is coming. As we reach solar grid parity, within ten years clean energy will be at a lower cost per kilowatt than fossil fuel energy. And, as Peter Diamandis argues in *Abundance*, soon we will have a world in which everyone globally has access to their basic needs.

After 200,000 years of *homo sapiens* being around, within the next 40 years we will for the first time in human history create a carbon-neutral sustainable world in which everyone has access to food, water, shelter, and education as well as modern medicine, electricity, and the cloud.

The four billion "digital natives" born between 1980 and 2015 intuitively understand global connection, species-level identity, and innovation and will be leading the time ahead—bringing exciting new perspectives to replace the industrial-age thinking of the past. We see business, when done right, as a tool for good. We see efficient, effective, transparent, and technologically-enabled government as essential.

In the two-hundred-year debate of socialism vs. capitalism, it is socially responsible capitalism that will win—built on a foundation of compassionate and efficiently-run cloud-enabled government and a connected electorate.

The companies that build a better world for all will prosper. The entrepreneurs who build companies that make a positive impact will prosper. The politicians who embrace the reality of a connected, interdependent world, driven by innovation and ubiquitous access to the cloud, will prosper.

We should celebrate this human achievement of the democratization of access to information, people, and opportunity—and push to bring the cloud to 100% of humanity by 2030. The cloud is the greatest innovation platform ever built. The cloud has come a long way from its origins as ARPANET in 1969.

The Innovation Age will be characterized by the transformative effects of a world with ubiquitous cloud-connected nanocomputers. Every human being will be empowered to learn, grow, and make a difference for their family, community, and world. Every business and every government will have to be re-imagined as we solve the challenges of the future, creating great opportunity for Millennial entrepreneurs and leaders.

For the leaders and innovators of tomorrow, the greatest opportunity is completing the work of our forebears and finally building a world that is both sustainable, with low-cost clean energy, and prosperous—a world in which all people have access to what they need to survive and thrive.

Imagine the innovation that will ensue when every person in the world has access to Wikipedia, Khan Academy, and Code Academy. This Innovation Age is coming. In this Innovation Age, everyone globally will be able to access and the best tools and software, often run on and powered by the mobile supercomputer in their pocket, eyeglasses, or contact lenses.

A sustainable, prosperous, and connected world is ahead. A world in which bad dictators get ousted, unethical leaders get exposed, people who harm others get put on broadcast streaming iTV. A world in which we all have access to education, knowledge, and information is coming. A world in which we have equal rights under internally enforced law, regardless of birthplace or skin color, is coming. A world in which everyone has enough to eat, enough clean water to drink, and access to medicine, lighting, and a solid roof over their head is coming. This world is not the one we live in yet—but wow, we've come a long way toward this world of sustainable global prosperity in the last 200 years.

What comes after the Innovation Age? We do not yet know. But perhaps it will be an Integral Age in which we are multi-planetary as a species, respect all forms of nature, and can extend life well beyond current limits.

Prosperous sustainability is coming. To achieve it will take your help and the collaboration of all of us.

The Mobile & Cloud World of 2014

The always-on Internet is recreating the world to be much more efficient and seamless as we build a global network of connected sensors and connected minds with a global human identity at its core.

The human race is being pushed forward. Together we are creating a better world. A sustainable world. A globally prosperous world. A connected world. A decentralized world in which despotic genocidal dictators can no longer gain the legitimacy needed for sustained power.

Connectivity in 1994 was a landline. Today it's a pair of glasses that can connect to 3 billion cloud users.

In the world of 1994 we had telephone booths, faxes, and desktop computers. In the world of 2014 we have cloud services for everything.

The world is moving from no-one having access, to only a few having access through direct-ownership, to everyone having access on-demand at a lower cost. No longer do we all need to own a car, records, and a video library.

All we need is a laptop, a smartphone, and the cloud and we can access any service anytime. Soon every government service too will be delivered via the mobile cloud.

You can monitor your heart rate and sleep via an Android smartwatch. You can check your blood sugar via bluetooth-enabled smart contact lenses. Every device will be connected to the cloud and managed remotely. The "internet of things," it is called. Beautiful and easy services are revolutionizing pretty much everything.

Here's a table contrasting the norms of 1994 with 2014, only 20 years later.

Category	1994	2014
Books	Printed	Kindle, iPad, Nook
Cameras	Film & Development	Device-Integrated, Synced to Cloud
Cars	Self-owned	GetAround, Zipcar, Lyft, Uber
Channel Changing	Remotes	Hand Gestures
Check Out	Cash Register	Square + Tablet
Citizen Action	Faxes, Calls	Change.org
Communication	Postal Mail, Fax, Landlines	Smartphones, Email, SMS, Facebook, Twitter, WhatsApp, SnapChat
Contact Management	Rolodexes	Connect, Google Contacts
Doctors Appointments	Phone Call	ZocDoc, One Medical
Event Planning	Mail & Telephone	EventBrite, Facebook Events, YPlan
Fashion	Expensive Boutiques	RentTheRunway, Gilt
Food Delivery	Phone Call	GrubHub, Munchery
Fitness	Gym	Nike FuelBand, FitBit, Jawbone Up, Basis
Funding	Friends & Funding	Kickstarter, Fundable, Indiegogo
Global Outsourcing	Plane travel	Crowdflower, Exec, ODesk, Elance, Guru, SmarterWork, Freelancer
GPS	Not available to consumers	GPS on your smartphone
Groceries	Local store	Amazon Fresh, Instacart
Information Storage	Storage Cabinets	DropBox, Box, Google Drive, SkyDrive
Job Searching	Fairs & Resumes	LinkedIn, The Ladders
Knowledge	Encyclopedia Britannica	Wikipedia, KhanAcademy, CodeAcademy, Udemy, SkillShare, Coursera, iTunes U
Lending	Banks	LendingClub, Prosper, Kabbage
Locks	Deadbolts	Lockitron
Maps	Printed	Google Maps, Bing Maps
Marketing	Direct mail, phone book, billboards	Paid search, social ads, mobile ads

Movies	Blockbuster	Netflix, Amazon, iTunes, YouTube, Hulu
Music	Cassettes & CDs	Spotify, Rdio
News	Television, Radio, & Newspaper	Twitter, Flipboard, Prismatic
Note Taking	Notepads	Evernote, Google Docs
Phones	Landlines	Smartphones
Picture Storage	Photo Albums	Facebook, Flickr, 500px
Plumber	Phone Book	HandyBook, Angie's List
Product Design	In-house	Quirky
Reviews	Word of Mouth	Yelp
Scrapbooks	Hand-created	Pinterest
Shopping	Mall	Amazon, eBay
Signatures	Pens & Fax	Docusign, EchoSign
Social Network	Bar, Alumni Reunion	Facebook, Instagram, Google+, LinkedIn
Task Management	Post-its	Trello, Asana
Tasks	Classifieds	TaskRabbit, Zaarly, Zirtual
Television	Cable & Bunny Ear Antennas	HuluPlus, Netflix, Apple TV, iTunes, Amazon Fire TV
Textbooks	Buy them at a bookstore	Chegg, Amazon Textbook Rental
Thermostats	Analog	Nest
Traffic-Information	Radio	Waze, Google Maps
Wallets	Leather	Google Wallet
Watches	Swatch & Rolex	Pebble, Basis

What a world of rapid innovation we live in! All this technological advancement in just twenty years.

What could you create in the next couple decades that might improve the world?

We'll end this chapter with four profiles of four of our favorite contemporary innovators.

- Jack Andraka - Born in 1997, by the age of 15 he has already changed the world with his innovation. Andraka has developed a new way to detect pancreatic, ovarian, and lung cancer during early stages when there is a much higher likelihood of a cure. His inexpensive method, which could save countless lives, won the 2012 Gordon E. Moore Award, the grand prize of the Intel International Science and Engineering Fair.

- **Eesha Khare** - Another impressive young innovator, who at the age of 18 created a tiny device that could charge a mobile phone in 20-30 seconds—a revolutionary technology she calls a "super-capacitor." She won the 2013 Intel Foundation Young Scientist Award for her invention, and plans to use the prize money to pay for her tuition at Harvard and continue her work as an inventor.

- **Jeffrey Grossman** - A professor at MIT in the field of nanotechnology and he recently showed how sheets of graphene, a one-atom-thick form of the element carbon, can be used to desalinate water. This innovation could potentially provide a cost effective solution to the increasing worldwide problem of a shortage of fresh water. He also produced an amazing course called "Understanding Science for Tomorrow," which is part of *The Great Courses* and available online to purchase.

- **Robert Pera** - An Apple hardware engineer who struck out on his own in 2005 with the goal of bringing affordable wireless internet access to the world's emerging markets. By the age of 34, Robert has created a public company, Ubiquiti Networks, worth nearly a billion dollars, that is bringing Internet access to developing world through Wi-max Wi-fi networks. He's truly bringing the cloud to the world and doing an amazing service while making a lot of money at the same time.

Ch 11. How to Use Your Life for Good

“ Something hit me very hard once, thinking about what one little man could do. Think of the Queen Mary — the whole ship goes by and then comes the rudder. And there's a tiny thing at the edge of the rudder called a trimtab. Just moving the little trimtab builds a low pressure that pulls the rudder around... The little individual can be a trimtab. Society thinks it's going right by you, that it's left you altogether. But if you're doing dynamic things mentally, the fact is that you can just put your foot out... and the whole big ship... is going to go. So I said, call me Trimtab.

—R. Buckminster Fuller

The Biggest Opportunities for Millennials

In the 1967 movie *The Graduate,* Mr. McGuire advises young Benjamin to go into the field of plastics for his career.

> **Mr. McGuire**: I want to say one word to you. Just one word.
> **Benjamin**: Yes, sir.
> **Mr. McGuire**: Are you listening?
> **Benjamin**: Yes, I am.
> **Mr. McGuire**: Plastics.
> **Benjamin**: Exactly how do you mean?
> **Mr. McGuire**: There's a great future in plastics. Think about it.

If plastics was the hot area to work in during 1967, what career fields should you consider dedicating the rest of your life to? And how can you both do what you love and love what you do?

We believe that you can make a huge impact regardless of which sector of the economy you work in--business, government, or non-profit. Whether you work in big business or entrepreneurship, science or journalism, activism or public service--we know you can make a huge impact. Ultimately, we want you to be able to do work that you love--and within a field that is exciting and with mentors from whom you can learn.

In this chapter, we'll look at seven broad areas of opportunity for Millennials that can be major areas of leverage for global impact and economic potential.

1. Energy & Environment
2. Food & Water
3. Education
4. Health & Wellness
5. Engineering
6. Financial Access
7. Computing

We'll start by looking at some of the biggest opportunities in the field of the energy and environment.

Energy & Environment

1. **Solar Energy** - We're currently seeing a Moore's Law-like effect in which the cost of solar power is being cut in half every two years. By 2020, solar power will be less expensive than power coming from the lowest cost fossil fuels. As of 2014, it costs about $0.20 per kilowatt hour of solar electricity at retail and $0.05 per kilowatt hour for grid electricity from natural gas. By 2020, it's projected that those two numbers will meet (called "Grid Parity") and solar power will be a lower cost than natural gas. The leading U.S. home solar installer is SolarCity and the leading U.S. photovoltaics manufacturer is First Solar.

2. **Advanced Batteries** - Solar power only works when the sun is out. Thus, we need new battery technologies to store up the electrical energy for the night like Ambri and Acquion and new electric car batteries like those from Boston Power.

3. **Biofuels** - Craig Venter's firm Synthetic Genomics is actively working in partnership with ExxonMobil to develop a synthesized version of algae that allows the large-scale low cost production of renewable biofuel.

4. **Climate Engineering** - David Keith & Andy Parker at Harvard are making substantial progress within the field of climate engineering. For an interesting take on the possible future effects of climate engineering gone wrong see "The Fate of An Engineered Planet" in the *Scientific American,* January 2013. One promising option for removing CO2 from the atmosphere is Bioenergy Carbon Capture and Storage (BECCS). The Swedish firm Biorecro is one of the leaders in this new field of BECCS.

5. **Sustainable City Planning** - in 2009 For the first time in human history, more humans lived in cities than in rural areas. One example of an innovator in this area is the city of Masdar in the UAE, which is now the world's first zero carbon city.

Food & Water

1. **Synthetic Food Production -** The world's first laboratory beef burger — a proof of concept after five years of research — was cooked and eaten in August 2013. The chief creator of the artificial patties was Mark Post of Maastricht University in the Netherlands. Synthetic meat has the potential to greatly reduce the inhumane slaughter of animals and enable low cost high protein food to be available globally.

2. **Agricultural Tech -** Technology that enables greater agricultural yields will be crucial in a world that must feed 9 billion. New methods of plant breeding and the expansion of perennial crop planting will help. Arduino-based farm sensors from Boston-based Apitronics are at the center of a new trend of combining cloud-connected sensors with farming.

3. **Vertical Farming -** Dickson Despommier, a professor of environmental health sciences and microbiology at Columbia University in New York City, modernized the idea of vertical farming---cultivating fruits and vegetables within a skyscraper greenhouse or on vertically inclined surfaces in order to reduce the need for land

4. **Water Desalination -** Recent research at MIT from The Grossman Group has used graphene to create a highly energy-efficient manner of removing salt from water. As the human population grows, ensuring access to clean water for all of us is critically important to enabling both human health and geopolitical stability.

Education

1. **Cloud Education -** Companies like Coursera, Udemy, Udacity, CodeAcademy, and SkillShare and non-profits like Khan Academy and EDx are enabling anyone around the world with self-motivation and a cloud connection to receive a Harvard, Stanford, or MIT-quality education.

2. **Low Cost Schooling -** NEA and Khosla Ventures backed Bridge International, based in Nairobi, Kenya, has created a new low cost education model in East Africa that costs just $4 per month per student. Their East African schools are nearing 100,000 enrolled students. Across the world in San Francisco new primary education company AltSchool, has raised $33 million from Founders Fund and Andreessen Horowitz to create an elementary school that is tech-enabled and student centered. In the future AltSchool hopes to be a lower cost, higher quality form of primary education around the world.

3. **Leadership Training -** Leadership training is a big business. And if you do it well you can sit at a major fulcrum point for leverage in global systems change. At Hive, we believe that if the leaders of the future

are taught purpose-driven leadership (leadership based on putting an authentic mission first) that a lot can change for the better.

4. **Network Building -** Training leaders is one thing. Connecting them in an authentic global community and network is another. We believe that there is a lot of opportunity in the field of building strong networks within and across professions and passions. With the explosion of digital social networks, there is tremendous opportunities in building the right kinds of in-person social networks.

Health & Wellness

1. **Synthetic Biology -** Biology once was solely the domain of nature. Now, humans have learned how to edit the code of life, with applications ranging from synthetic algae smartfuels, to synthetic food that can feed billions, to altered stem cells that can extend life. To learn more, check out the book *Re-Genesis: How Synthetic Biology Will Reinvent Nature and Ourselves* by Ed Regis.

2. **Brain Mapping -** We are now beginning to understand how the neurons of the brain connect and work together to enable learning and memory. Take a look at the research from The Connectome Project, a $38.5M project. In 2013, the U.S. government announced $100M in funds for brain mapping research in a new effort called The BRAIN Initiative. Young genius David Dalrymple, while at MIT and Harvard, has worked on unraveling the neuron connections for the nematode worm. To learn more about this field of both mapping the human brain and recreating the human brain see the book *How to Create a Mind* by Ray Kurzweil.

3. **Optogenetics -** Researchers from Stanford recently showed the ability to control the brain of a mouse through light emitting diodes. The process uses light to manipulate specially treated neurons inside the brain. Optogenetics may prove helpful in treating Parkinson's,

Alzheimer's, and Multiple Sclerosis.

4. **Reverse Aging -** 2011 research from Dr. Gary Lynch at UC-Irvine has explored the connection between Ampakines and amplifying the electricity between neurons to enable you to think like you were young again.

5. **Personalized Medicine -** Following the completion of the Human Genome Project and the full sequencing of human DNA, companies like 23&Me have advanced the field of personal gene sequencing. For just $99, you can get your DNA partially sequenced, enabling you to better understand your ancestry and risk of diseases.

6. **Bionic Eyesight -** The first Bionic Eye implant, made by California-based Second Sight with support from the Department of Energy, in late 2013 became medically available in the United States for patients blinded by retinitis pigmentosa, or RP, a degenerative eye disease that affects 1 in 4,000 Americans.

7. **Low-cost Sanitation -** Whether it be soap from Unilever or new low-cost toilet systems for the developing world like those from Sanergy and Toilets for People, sanitation is big business--and critical to the health and welfare of humanity.

8. **Mindfulness Training -** One of Google's earliest engineers was named Chade-Meng Tan. Meng, as he is known, went on to create the Search Inside Yourself program within Google that has now become its own company and organization, taking mindfulness and meditation practices to the most influential tech companies in Silicon Valley. A world away in Kuala Lumpur, the company MindValley has created the world's largest meditation app Omvana. Well known global organizations that teach mindfulness, holistic yoga, and meditation worldwide include Art of Living and the Isha Foundation.

Engineering

1. **Clean transportation** - Elon Musk's Tesla has been a pioneer in the field of electric cars, creating the first new profitable American car company in decades. Elon's new idea of the Hyperloop could enable fast, clean transportation that takes you from San Francisco to LA in under 30 minutes (or SF to NYC in 1 hour) at speeds of up to 6,400 kph using magnetic levitation.

2. **Self-Driving Cars -** Both Tesla and Google are working on building a self-driving car. In Masdar, UAE (the "City of the Future") electronic automated transport cars (called Podcars) are used underground to enable rapid transport as part of their initiative to build a zero-carbon city.

3. **Robotics -** Professor Hiroshi Ishiguro has created a robot twin called Geminoid. Geminoid uses motion capture sensors and sophisticated actuators to replicate every move down to the smallest twitch. The company Boston Dynamics has also created a number of advanced robots in partnership with DARPA.

4. **Private Space Exploration -** Companies like SpaceX and Virgin Galactic are working hard on enabling commercial space travel. By 2025, anyone with $100,000 will be able to go into space. By 2050, anyone with $5,000 will be able to take the trip. According to my friends at the Mars Climate Modeling Group at NASA Ames, we'll embark on our first human mission to Mars around 2025 and be an interplanetary species within our lifetime.

5. **3D Printing -** Five years ago, 3D printers were out of reach except for large companies. Today anyone with $1300 can purchase a Cubify 3D printer and print thousands of objects on-demand, ranging from forks, to artwork, to iPhone cases, to jewelry. Companies like 3D Systems and Bespoke System are even 3D printing artificial limbs and jaws.

6. **Nanotechnology -** Nanotechnology (a subset of the field of materials sciences) is enabling substantial innovations in areas ranging from carbon nanotubes to graphene-based water desalination to 3D printing

with claytronics. To learn more about nanotech, check out MIT Professor Jeffrey Grossman's nanotechnology videos within the course Understanding the Science for Tomorrow.

7. **Super Long-life Batteries -** New smartphones are more powerful than top of the line desktop computers from less than a decade ago. Battery life remains a continued issue for these more powerful handheld supercomputers. Research advances from NASA in long-life plutonium-238 batteries, used in applications like the Mars Curiosity Rover and pacemakers, hold promise for a future of laptop and phone batteries that last 10 years--the holy grail for the business traveller.

8. **Low Cost Housing -** In a world where millions of people are forced from their houses every year because of natural disasters, there is an ongoing need for huge numbers of decent mid- to long-term temporary housing units that can be swiftly delivered to the affected area. The Reaction Housing System has been developed to make the wait as short as possible.

Financial Access

1. **Mobile Banking -** Mobile banking is finally becoming commonplace in the USA with leaders like Simple, recently acquired by Spain's BBVA for $117M.

2. **Frontier Market Finance -** In the developing world, Accion in Latin America and M-Pesa and Kopo Kopo in Kenya have been three highlights in the financial services sector. In Africa, for example, there are over 1.1 billion consumers across 54 countries. The banks and technologies that support the infrastructural growth of the African continent stand to make a lot of money, and impact, in the 21st century.

3. **Payment Processing -** Companies like Intuit, Square, eBay's Paypal, and Venmo (owned by Paypal) have made it a whole lot easier to send money to a friend or pay for a product at a local store. Cash registers

are so 1999.

4. **Digital Currency** - Created by an anonymous person using the pseudonym Satoshi Nakamoto in 2008, Bitcoin is a peer-to-peer digital currency based on cryptography. Bitcoins are mined using computer servers that execute complex cryptographic algorithms that become increasingly complex. The value of one bitcoin ranged from $2.32 to $1132 in its first five years of trading. Bitcoin has been the first digital currency to gain widespread awareness.

5. **Digital Wallets -** Paypal, Google Wallet, Apple Passport, Square Wallet, Isis, and Lemon Wallet are all competing to make the 20th centuryesque physical leather container in your pocket or purse, well, a relic of the 20th century. A clear leader is yet to emerge.

Computing

1. **Quantum Computing -** In 2013, Google purchased a DWAVE II Quantum Computer and in partnership with the NASA Ames Research Center, created the Quantum Artificial Research Center (QUAIL). Unlike binary computers, in which bits must be in either the 1 state or the 0 state, quantum computers use superposition to enable all states between 0 and 1, enabling faster computation of some key computer processes.

2. **Converged Smartphones -** Wonderfully, your smartphone will soon also be your desktop PC. You'll simply plug your phone into an HDMI monitor to turn it into a full desktop computer. Once smartphones are powerful enough to run Excel, there will be no reason to have a separate computer unit for the larger monitor. The Ubuntu Edge Project is perhaps the best example so far of this concept of "frames" and desktop-ready phones.

3. **DNA Data Storage -** Recent work at Harvard has enabled the storing of data within DNA, storing 700 terabytes of data into a single gram of

DNA. In 2012, <u>IBM announced it could store a bit of data on just 12 atoms</u>. Data storage is being revolutionized nearly yearly as more and more data is able to be stored and analyzed and as more people and more devices join the cloud.

4. **Artificial Intelligence -** In 2011 <u>IBM Watson</u> beat prior champions Ken Jennings and Brad Rutter in Jeopardy. Now, IBM is using the Watson technology to help doctors diagnose patients. In the next forty years, AI-enabled machine-learning robots and devices will have many applications as humans and technology continue to merge.

5. **Contact Lens Smartphones -** Dr. Babak Parviz is in charge of Project Glass at Google. Before Project Glass, Dr. Parviz was working on contact lens smartphones at the University of Washington. Someday, you'll be able to surf the internet and communicate with your friends with an <u>electronic contact lens</u>. Companies like <u>Innovega</u> are working hard on creating a communication device that can be worn directly in your eyes.

6. **Natural User Interfaces -** Natural user interfaces include touch, voice, hand gesture, and thought. The iPhone brought multi-touch interaction to the masses beginning in 2007. Siri brought voice interaction to the masses in 2010. <u>LeapMotion</u> is bringing hand gesture interaction to the masses now. <u>Emotiv</u> is bringing thought control to computer interfaces. The NUI revolution in computing is just beginning, and will be as big of a shift in human-computer interaction as the move to Graphical User Interfaces (GUIs) in the 1980s.

7. **Government 2.0 -** Imagine every Federal Government agency having a real-time Geckoboard dashboard in its lobby, enabling transparency and a focus on results and efficiency in government. Imagine a Department of Motor Vehicles (DMV) in which you submit your digital birth certificate, a picture, and digital social security card via an iPhone app and then have your new license FedEx'd to you overnight. These changes will be coming to Washington in the next two decades. The work that U.S. CTO Todd Park and U.S. CIO Steve VanRoekel are doing

to open up access to data and create accountability and transparency in government is just the beginning.

8. **Cybersecurity -** In a world of Government-driven cyberattacks (like the U.S. Stuxnet attack on Iranian nuclear facilities in 2010), the world of cybersecurity will be a very, very large market in the decades ahead.

9. **Wearable Computers** - Wearable devices and Heads-Up Displays are becoming more and more common. Entrants range from Basis and Pebble watches, to the self-quantifying JawBone Up and Nike's FuelBand, to the cloud-connected HUDs like Google Glass, GlassUp, Oakley's Airwaves, and Oculus VR headsets, being developed as a subsidiary of Facebook.

10. **Implantable Computers -** Pacemakers, cochlear implants, bionic eyes, and synthetic organs already exist. Electronic devices and synthetic materials have already begun to merge with the human body. This trend will accelerate in the years ahead, enabling rapid advances in human health while also bringing up both critical ethical issues and human rights issues. To learn more, check out *The Singularity is Near* and *The Transcendent Man*.

11. **The Internet of Things -** In the future, cloud-connected chips and sensors will be in everyday devices. These devices will be interlinked, creating an "Internet of Things." It won't just be your television, tablet, and phone that are connected. Also connected will be your thermostat, car, fridge, pacemaker, and teddy bear. Field-of-vision smart phones may someday even be able to be installed non-invasively through our capillaries and connect into our optic nerve.

12. **Mobile Software -** Accordinging to Gartner, in 2014, the Android OS will ship on over 1 billion new devices while Apple's iOS will be on over 350 million. Building software for Android and iOS mobile devices is one of the biggest businesses this decade. By building the new tools that will power mobile consumers and professionals, you have the

opportunity to influence the daily habits and behaviors of hundreds of millions of people while making a global impact.

Technology is accelerating. Understand it. Prepare yourself. And be sure to position your life's work within a field that has the promise to bring great benefit to humanity.

Recommended Chapter Resources:

- Slides: _Kleiner Perkins Internet Trends 2013_ by Mary Meeker and Liang Wu
- Book: _How to Create a Mind_ by Ray Kurzweil
- Book: _The Singularity is Near_ by Ray Kurzweil
- Video: _The Transcendent Man_

Ch 11. Creating The Future

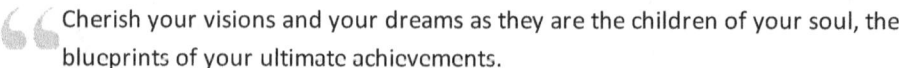 Cherish your visions and your dreams as they are the children of your soul, the blueprints of your ultimate achievements.

—*Napoleon Hill*

The World in 2050

An artists depiction of Masdar, the world's first carbon neutral city, under construction presently in the United Arab Emirates

In order to talk about the future of the world, we have to project some important statistics so that we can at least understand what is likely to be seen in the future. In this section, we'll be using some data from the Pardee Center for International Futures to highlight some trends that are going on at the macro level and projecting them forward to 2050.

Let's start by looking at population. For tens of thousands of years, human population was stuck at under a billion people. Around 1800, we start to see the beginning of a rapid increase in human population as we hit the industrial age. With new innovations and new abilities to produce food at scale, we have been able to increase the global population from about 1 billion to a little over 7 billion in the last couple of hundred years.

In the next 35 years, the UN estimates that we're going to see population rise above 9 billion and then begin to level off. This will create new market opportunities for entrepreneurs all over the world, but it will also create new challenges for governments in metropolises and cities, and particularly for folks that are working on environmental issues. Global energy demands will more than double by 2050. Fossil fuel usage fortunately will peak and then decline as we begin to move to more renewables.

Looking at Internet access, broadband is expected to reach 85% of the population by 2050, up from about 9% as of 2010. We actually think the number will be closer to 100%. That is an exciting trend. When we can get high speed access combined with pocket supercomputers in the hands of more than 80% of the world, amazing things will happen.

In terms of life expectancy, we'll continue to improve. In the last 40 years, human life expectancy has increased from 59 to over 70. In the next 40 years, life expectancy is on track to go from 70 to 77, about a 10% improvement. Based on some of the medical science coming out of Silicon Valley, particularly at Singularity University and at Stanford, we would not be at all surprised if this number actually gets blown out of the water and that average life expectancy is much beyond 80 by that time, if not more.

In terms of infant mortality, the great news is that fewer babies will die before age five, going from a global average over 30 (out of every thousand births) today to a global average under 10 (or under 1% of the population) by 2050.

The Future of Income and Poverty

In terms of economics, real GDP per capita (or average income per person) is likely to double over the next 40 years, from $10,000 today to about $18,000 in current dollars by 2050.

What's going to happen to extreme poverty? Well, we don't exactly know, but the Pardee Center believes that extreme poverty is going to go down from about 17% today to under 6% by 2050. We are passionate about creating a world without poverty, a world in which every human being has access to basic human needs and has the ability to create and inspire others and innovate.

We believe that extreme poverty can, in our lifetimes, asymptotically approach zero—probably by 2030-2035, if we as a species determine that having a world in which everyone has access to basic human needs is a priority.

When we create a world in which everyone has access to what they need to survive, what they need to raise their family, what they need to educate their kids and keep their families healthy, we will have a much more secure world in which all of us will be able to be more prosperous.

The May 2000 cover of *The Economist* referred to Africa as "The Hopeless Continent." We were very glad to see the same magazine, in its December 4, 2011 issue, writing a new story for Africa—a story of Africa rising. Africa is a continent that is rapidly growing, with tremendous opportunities. And that's true not just in Kenya, Uganda, and Rwanda but all over Africa—from Nigeria to Ghana to Botswana to South Africa. Investing in Africa today is a lot like investing in India or China 30 years ago before their major growth decades.

The Future of Education & Cities

In terms of education, we are going to be getting better educated as a species. We're going to go from a world in which 24% of the population finish secondary school to a world in which 46% of the population finish secondary school. It's a disturbing statistic: only one in four human beings today finish secondary schooling. But fortunately that's going to nearly double over the next 40 years.

In terms of college completion, globally it's around 7% today. But the percentage of people with college degrees over the next 40 years is going to triple to over 20% of the population. Imagine a world in which three times as many people had college degrees. I think that's going to be a better world.

And importantly, women will be going to college in droves, going from 5% of the population today to over 21% of the population in 2050—up nearly 3.5 times or a 265% increase.

Of course, the challenge in the 21st century is not to create obedient automatons incapable of original thought but rather engender creativity, innovation, the connection of dots across specialities, and the ability to synthesize diverse sets of information into a understanding of how the world works.

We're also becoming more urban as a species. We're moving from rural areas to suburban and urban areas. The percentage of our population in cities, which has just recently passed 50%, is likely to go 67% by 2050, according to the Pardee Center.

So in the next 35 years, we're going to see amazing innovations. We're going to see tremendous changes in the interactions of internal, external, and ecological systems. We have an exciting future ahead of us—one that I'm optimistic about.

Yes, we do have challenges, particularly with global security, nuclear proliferation, carbon output, and climate change, but we have an opportunity in the next 40 years, as global population expands beyond 9 billion people and science, technology, and the Internet are able to be democratized, to create an amazing future together. We're going to see some game-changing innovations in the years ahead, including nanotechnology, 3D printing, genome sequencing, synthetic life, private space travel, and new desalination techniques that can efficiently provide clean water to everyone.

The Future of Government

Governments will have to adapt to this new world. Societies and populations are going to demand increased government transparency, better access to public and government data, and stronger property rights.

For innovation to spread globally, it's going to need to get easier to start a business around the world. We're going to need better and smarter regulations on carbon dioxide output. Some of the remaining totalitarian and authoritarian regimes that don't listen to their populations are likely to be overthrown now that their populations have technologies that enable anyone to easily communicate with a massive group of people, en masse, and create group action that catalyzes change.

Fortunately, with social media, we're entering a world in which if you are not a transparent person, if you're not an authentically good person, you will not be able to be elected as a leader because people will know and that information will get out. We're moving into a world where, if you want to be a leader, you have to be a good person. I look forward to that world.

Major geopolitical changes are going to happen as well. It's projected that by the mid-2020s China will have the world's largest GDP. India will be the world's most populous nation. Africa, which today is the stage for some of the most extreme poverty in the world, will have over 2 billion people and be a true economic power, a market of two-ninths of the world in which there are tremendous moves ahead as they leapfrog some of the technologies that we've built here in the West.

Fossil fuel producers will have less influence as we begin to move away from fossil fuels pretty quickly, out of necessity. We will have continued insecurity globally until we lower our emissions, particularly considering that some of the most significant and dangerous effects of climate change are going to happen in the places that currently have the least economic security. If we truly want a secure, prosperous, strong economy and a strong society, we need to take fossil fuel reduction and the move to clean renewable energy very seriously.

Ch 13. The Millennial Opportunity

> When you grow up you tend to get told the world is the way it is and your life is just to live your life inside the world. Try not to bash into the walls too much. Try to have a nice family life, have fun, save a little money. That's a very limited life. Life can be much broader once you discover one simple fact, that everything around you that you call life, was made up by people who were no smarter than you. Once you learn that, you'll never be the same again.
>
> —Steve Jobs, 1994

How Millennials Are Different

Millennials will be leading the next 30 years. We define Millennials as people who were born between 1980 and 2000. In 2045, the youngest millennials will be about 45 and the oldest millennials will be about 65. As we see the Internet generation grow up and become leaders with all this access to information and knowledge , we're going to see amazing, positive changes in society. But we also have great challenges ahead of us that we have to tackle head on.

The Millennial generation is a different generation than those that have come before in many ways. Most notably, the advent of the Internet and our ability to communicate with each other globally like never before has given us the ability to connect to each other like no prior generation.

Let's look at what's different about this Millennial generation.

1. **We Are Deeply Aware of Social Issues -** We are able to access information from around the world like never before. We've seen since the mid-1990s that we've had access to the Internet really from the beginning of our life, or at least from our early teenage years. We're aware of what's going on in the world and more globally connected.

2. **We Understand the Importance of Sustainability -** We understand the importance of a sustainable world, a world in which we can leave a tremendously positive future for our grandchildren.

3. **We See Business & Entrepreneurship as a Good Thing -** We see business and entrepreneurship not as tools of evil capitalists, but as tools to make scalable, positive change in the world. We see conscious capitalism as a change in capitalism that doesn't look at creating short-term quarter-by-quarter profit results as its primary objective, but rather thinks about creating value for society. And when you create value for society, for customers, for employees, for community, you actually end up creating lots of shareholder value. We see that social responsibility and economic returns actually are positively

correlated rather than tradeoffs.

4. **We're Used to a Faster Pace of Change -** We have so much information coming at us through so many different media outlets all at the same time that we can multi-task quite well and we're often impatient with the status quo because we believe we can do anything. We believe we can truly change the world, and together we have the ability, resources, and technologies to make change faster than ever before. That brings with it an important requirement that we take time to talk to each other, to connect and make sure we make the right changes, but we're used to a faster pace of change. We don't like bureaucracy.

5. **We're Globally Connected Like Never Before -** Through technology, we're globally connected like never before. We can now jump on Facebook or WeChat and talk with a friend in Syria or Egypt, or even a friend in South Korea or Iran. We have the ability to connect with people globally, regardless of where they are. The reality is young people are the same everywhere. Human beings just want the same thing, and that's to live a good life with opportunity and be able to take care of our families and create a better world for our kids than the world that we lived in. We all share the same goals. And really, at the end of the day, we're all humans. As we realize that by becoming globally connected and creating a sense of human identity, we believe we'll be able to create a more peaceful, stronger, more secure world for all.

6. **We Have the Tools & Confidence to Topple Corrupt Leaders**
    We also now have the tools to topple corrupt leaders and hold bad leaders accountable. We've seen with the Arab Spring in 2011 the leaders of countries like Egypt, Tunisia, and Libya all be overthrown just within about a six or nine-month period. We are seeing that today with tools like Change.org, Twitter, Facebook, and Google that we can connect, communicate, interact, and organize like never before. One of the great principles the United States was founded on was people

should not be afraid of their governments; governments should be afraid of their people. We are excited by the amount of grassroots activism that is now possible.

Our Biggest Opportunity

Our biggest challenge, and our biggest opportunity as a generation, is creating once and for all an environmentally sustainable world in which everyone all around the world has access to the basic needs of food, water, shelter, education, medicine, electricity, and the cloud.

The great news is our generation cares and are deeply passionate. We give a damn and we have the tech know-how. We can innovate like hell and we're highly competent. We've excited about what the leaders of our generation will create in the decades ahead.

So, what then is your opportunity?

Well, you have the opportunity to co-create the future. That's pretty awesome.

For the first time, we have a generation that is connected across borders that can work together to create a world that is sustainable and abundant for all people--not just for some people.

We hope that you'll make the conscious choice to use your life to contribute to humanity, however you best can. We hope you will choose to live a life that is driven by compassion for all people and all species. And we hope that wherever you live, you'll join a global community of people working to make a difference, whether it is the World Economic Forum Global Shapers, Sandbox, Hive, or many others that are springing up. This work is best done together, not alone.

We hope that you'll choose to live a joyous life of purpose and passion rather than a stress-filled life of worry. We hope that you'll choose to live a life in which you do what you love, and love what you do. As Howard Thurman said, what the world needs is people who have "come alive" and who can contribute their greatest gifts to humanity.

We believe that in our lifetime together we can create a world that is sustainable, abundant, and joyous for all people. We'd love to work with you to make that happen. We are one team.

As Donella Meadows, the great MIT systems theorist would say, find your place of leverage in the system and make your difference.

We are entering a new age. An exciting new age. Great wisdom will be needed as the pace of change quickens.

Here at Hive, we'd like to co-create the future along with you. We invite you to join our community of people who are working to create a better world at www.hive.org.

Recommended Chapter Resources:

- Video: Creating a Global Movement by Jenny Sauer-Klein
- Video: The One Project by Justin Rosenstein
- PDF: "Leverage Points, Places to Intervene in a System" by Donella Meadows
- PDF: "The Never Ending Upward Quest" by Jessica Roemischer
- Video: "The Prophecy of the Eagle and the Condor" by John Perkins

Appendix: Recommended Resources

Recommended Courses

Art of Living - Happiness Program - www.artofliving.org
A four-day course on happiness, yoga, and mindfulness that teaches a meditation technique called the Sudarshan Kriya. Available in hundreds of cities globally.

Camp Grounded - www.campgrounded.com
An extremely fun three day summer camp for adults held in Northern California.

Esalen - www.esalen.org
A beautiful retreat center in Big Sur, California founded in 1962 designed to guide individuals through the exploration of their full potential. Offers reflection retreats and teacher-led courses.

Hive - Global Leaders Program - www.hive.org
A three-day program for people 21-39 who want to make a positive impact in the world. Designed to connect you with others who want to make a difference and give you clarity on your life plan.

ISHA Foundation - Inner Engineering - www.ishafoundation.org
A three day course on meditation, yoga, and mindfulness. Available in the USA and India or online at http://www.innerengineering.com/ieo/.

Landmark - The Landmark Forum -www.landmarkworldwide.com
A three-day course on living an extraordinary life. Available in many cities globally. Also recommended is the Landmark Advanced Course and Self-Expression & Leadership Program.

Singularity University - Executive Program - www.singularityu.org
A week long course for executives on the future of science and technology at the NASA Ames Campus in Mountain View, CA.

Starting Bloc - www.startingbloc.org
A five-day program for people 21-30 who want to make a positive impact on the world. Hosted in four major U.S. cities annually.

Recommended Books

- *Abundance* by Peter Diamandis
- *Creative Confidence* by Tom and David Kelly
- *Change by Design* by Tim Brown
- *Man's Search for Meaning* by Victor Frankl
- *Sophie's World* by Jostein Gaarder
- *The Art of Happiness* by The Dalai Lama
- *The Commanding Heights* by Daniel Yergin
- *The Future of Life* by E.O. Wilson
- *The Rational Optimist by* Matt Ridley
- *The Worldly Philosophers* by Ron Heilbroner

Book Contributors

Creating a Better World being co-created and edited by the members of the Hive Global Leaders program. Anyone from around the world can add comments at http://bit.ly/hivebook.

This is a list of the individuals who have made substantial contributions editing or commenting on this first version of the book.

Ryan Allis
Kate Clopeck
James Hanusa
Nadia Mufti
Rob Phillips
Adam Pumm
Michael Simmons
Matt Yazzie
David Wistocki

Endnotes

1. "Water, Sanitation and Hygiene." *UNICEF*. N.p., n.d. Web. 16 Apr. 2014.
2. "World Food Programme Fighting Hunger Worldwide." *Hunger Statistics*. N.p., n.d. Web. 14 Apr. 2014.
3. *The Right to Adequate Housing Fact Sheet*. Rep. Vol. 21. N.p.: UNHCR, n.d. Ser. 1. Web. 16 Apr. 2014.
   <http://www.ohchr.org/Documents/Publications/FS21_rev_1_Housing_en.pdf>.
4. "Access to Essential Medicines." *The World Medicines Situation*. World Health Organization, n.d. Web. 16 Apr. 2014.
5. *Adult and Youth Literacy*. Rep. N.p.: UNESCO Institute for Statistics, 2011. Web. 16 Apr. 2014. <http://www.uis.unesco.org/FactSheets/Documents/FS16-2011-Literacy-EN.pdf>.
6. "Internet Users as Percentage of Population." *World Bank*. Google Public Data Explorer, n.d. Web. 16 Apr. 2014.
   <http://www.google.com/publicdata/explore?ds=d5bncppjof8f9_&ctype=l&met_y=is_v eh_pcar_p3#!ctype=l&strail=false&bcs=d&nselm=h&met_y=it_net_user_p2&scale_y=lin &ind_y=false&rdim=region&ifdim=region&tdim=true&hl=en_US&dl=en_US&ind=false>.
7. *World Energy Outlook*. Rep. N.p.: IEA, 2011. Web. 16 Apr. 2014.
   <http://www.worldenergyoutlook.org/media/weowebsite/2011/executive_summary.p df>
8. *First Lady Eleanor Roosevelt Address the United Nations and Carnegie Hall*. Educational Video Group, 22 Oct. 2009. Web. 16 Apr. 2014.
   <https://www.youtube.com/watch?v=_6YNIXPGXKo>.
9. "Planck Reveals an Almost Perfect Universe." *European Space Agency*. N.p., n.d. Web. 18 Apr. 2014.
   <http://www.esa.int/Our_Activities/Space_Science/Planck/Planck_reveals_an_almost_p erfect_Universe>.
10. "Handwritten Draft of Albert Einstein's Letter to Robert S. Marcus (February 12, 1950)." *Flickr*. Albert Einstein Archives, Hebrew University of Jerusalem, Israel, n.d. Web. 18 Apr. 2014.
    <https://www.flickr.com/photos/speakingoffaith/4090564390/in/photostream/>.
11. "History of the World in Two Hours." *YouTube*. The History Channel, 23 Sept. 2012. Web. 18 Apr. 2014. <https://www.youtube.com/watch?v=qdLFCz1Y508>.
12. "World History Encyclopedia" P. 249, Web. 18 Apr. 2014.
    <http://books.google.fr/books?id=LEqaIGsT8SsC&pg=PA250&dq=Obsidian+trade&hl=fr &sa=X&ei=fDrWT6z-C_KY0QW_x_GFBA&ved=0CF0Q6AEwBg#v=onepage&q=Obsidian%2 0trade>.
13. Davies, Glyn; A History of money from ancient times to the present day, 3rd. ed. Cardiff: University of Wales Press, 2002. 720p.
14. Mortimer, Chambers; Hanawalt, Barbara, et al. *The Western Experience*, 8 th ed. New York: McGraw-Hill, 2003. pp 474.

15. Heilbroner, Robert L. *The Worldly Philosophers*. Page 25-31. New York: Touchstone. 1999.

16. "National Economic Accounts." *Bureau of Economic Analysis*. N.p., n.d. Web. 17 Apr. 2014. <http://www.bea.gov/national/index.htm#gdp>.

17. "Korean War." *Wikipedia*. Wikimedia Foundation, 16 Apr. 2014. Web. 16 Apr. 2014. <http://en.wikipedia.org/wiki/Korean_War>.

18. Berger, Marilyn. "Http://www.nytimes.com/2007/04/23/world/europe/23cnd-yeltsin.html." New York Times, 23 Apr. 2007. Web. 18 Apr. 2014. <http://www.nytimes.com/2007/04/23/world/europe/23cnd-yeltsin.html>.

19. The Commanding Heights, Episode 2, The Agony of Reforms, 19 min 14 sec

20. Zuse, Horst. "The Life and Work of Konrad Zuse." N.p., n.d. Web. 18 Apr. 2014. <http://web.archive.org/web/20100430212440/http://www.epemag.com/zuse/part1.htm>.

21. World Health Organization Global Health Histories

22. Life Expectancy - World Bank Public Data Explorer

23. 1900 Figure: Charles Kenny, A Century of the Infant Mortality Revolution, p. 13

24. Mortality rate, first year of life - World Bank Public Data Explorer

25. Angus Maddison, "Global Per Capita Income in 1900" ($1261 figure re-calibrated for 1990-2005 inflation to allow comparability).

26. World Bank, GDP per capita, PPP (constant 2005 international $),

27. Extreme Poverty Defined as Living Under $1.25 Per Day (in 2005 Dollars). Bourguignon and Morrison, Inequality Among World Citizens 1820-1992, Table 1 (midpoint between 1890 and 1910 figures), The American Economic Review.

28. World Bank, State of the Poor (1.2 billion / 7.1 billion)

29. 56% in 1950 per UNESCO, Mapping the Global Literacy Challenge p 165. Estimated at 42% by author taking into account Table 8.1 of developing country literacy rates in 1900 per UNESCO and the 1850 estimate of 10%, The Making of Literate Societies, pp. 189 and 192.

30. UNESCO Institute for Statistics, Adult and Youth Literacy Fact Sheet

31. Kim, Jim: Let's Be The Generation That Ends Poverty - April 2013 Post on LinkedIn

32. Proceedings of the National Academy of Sciences of the United States, High Income Improves Evaluation of Life But Not Emotional Well-Being, August 2010.